Praise for

"This book presents a unique account of Nigeria's fight against the COVID-19 pandemic. NCDC emerged from that experience as a beacon of hope in our nation's darkest hours. This book provides a narrative of resilience, diplomacy, and the collective effort against a common challenge. It serves as a reminder of the highs, lows, and unwavering spirit that enabled our country's response to an unprecedented global crisis. I am left with even deeper admiration and respect, for those at the frontline of our country's health security."
—**Yemi Osinbajo GCON**, *Vice President of Nigeria (2015 – May 2023)*

"This book provides a compelling narrative of Nigeria's COVID-19 response, as told through Chikwe's unique lens as DG of the Nigeria Centre for Disease Control. I commend this book for its exploration of Nigeria's resilient response—a true testament to collaborative efforts, leadership, and the unwavering spirit that influenced an entire nation facing a global crisis. I recommend this book to leaders across the world aspiring to strengthen their country's health security, as it provides valuable insights to navigate health challenges."
—**Tedros Adhanom Ghebreyesus**, *Director-General of the World Health Organization*

"*An Imperfect Storm* is a riveting account of the battle against COVID-19 by one of Nigeria's frontline heroes in that battle, Chikwe Ihekweazu and his wife and partner Vivianne. But the book is much more than that. It is also a fascinating journey through multiple facets of the national and global public health landscape. Told through a personal and biographical lens that weaves in the couple's love story, it is a read that once started is difficult to put down. I strongly recommend it to all those seeking to learn more about infectious disease control and management whilst enjoying a compelling narrative."

—**Ngozi Okonjo-Iweala**, *Director-General, World Trade Organization*

"*An Imperfect Storm* is an excellent playbook on leadership in an African context and a powerful guide to building a resilient African institution. It should be mandatory reading for anyone grappling with either. But more than anything it's a testament to Chikwe's incredible love for country and his strong and uncompromising sense of duty. We owe him."

—**Moky Makura**, *Executive Director, Africa No Filter*

"*An Imperfect Storm* is such an apt title for the heroic efforts of a few patriots like Chikwe Ihekweazu who had to guide Nigeria through what many feared would be a monumental COVID-19 crisis. Books like this must be written in order to help capture the capacity of some professionals like this author to impose and maintain standards against all odds."

—**Atedo Peterside CON**, *President & Founder of Anap Foundation & Chairman of the Anap Foundation COVID-19 Think Tank*

"I cannot think of anyone whose life will not be enriched by reading this book, a classic in every sense of the word. What a debt we owe Chikwe and Vivianne for sharing their stories with the world!"

—**Ike Anya**, *Author, Small by Small: Becoming a Doctor in 1990s Nigeria*

AN IMPERFECT STORM

A PANDEMIC AND THE COMING OF AGE OF A NIGERIAN INSTITUTION

A Memoir

Chikwe Ihekweazu

With Vivianne Ihekweazu

MASOBE

First published in 2024 by Masobe
An imprint of Masobe Books and Logistics Limited
34 Gbajumo Close, off Adeniran Ogunsanya,
Surulere, Lagos, Nigeria
Tel: +234 903 097 1752, +234 701 838 3286
Email: info@masobebooks.com

ISBN: 978-978-60488-9-5

Jacket design by Anderson Ofuzim Oriahi

Printed in India

www.masobebooks.com

To our sons Ginika and Barack (BBFL)
and our parents, Umelobi and Edith,
Lawrence and Azuka.

CONTENTS

ATTENUATION

FULL CIRCLE

FOREWORD

I still remember that phone call from Chikwe in February 2020. His tone, usually composed and measured, carried a sense of urgency as he conveyed the news—the first confirmed case of COVID-19 in Nigeria.

As the former leader of the Africa CDC, I had the privilege of observing firsthand the remarkable journey of Chikwe Ihekweazu at the Nigeria Centre for Disease Control (NCDC). From the onset in January 2017, as we commenced the process of operationalising the Africa CDC, I had the opportunity to collaborate closely with Chikwe as he had a similar task but at a national level shaping NCDC. In addition to the necessary work interactions, Chikwe and I developed a close allyship and brotherhood as we sought each other's counsel and support on critical issues, while never breaking the trust and confidence that came with this. Chikwe's narrative in this book is not just an individual's story; it encapsulates the very essence of transformation and resilience that we, as public health leaders, aspire to foster and cultivate across the continent and globally.

Amidst the challenges of the COVID-19 pandemic, NCDC's journey stands as a testament to leadership, resilience, and the capacity for transformation in the face of adversity. When Chikwe was appointed to lead NCDC in 2016, little did he know that he was steering towards a challenge that would redefine his role and chart a new course for public health in Africa's most populous country.

An Imperfect Storm written by Chikwe with the support of his amiable wife, Vivianne takes readers on an intimate journey of Nigeria's response to the COVID-19 pandemic, offering a deeply personal narrative of their experiences and the intricate challenges they faced. This book is not merely a memoir; it is a compelling chronicle of leadership, enterprise, and service in the heart of Africa, breaking the mould of commonly portrayed stories and unveiling a narrative that's often left untold.

As you go through the pages, the story of Nigeria's response to the pandemic emerges. Chikwe's narrative illustrates a tale of transformation and growth—from a medical student with aspirations in surgery to a leader navigating the complex world of outbreaks across the UK, Germany, and South Africa. His unexpected transition to the helm of Nigeria's national public health institute and the subsequent response to the pandemic narrate a journey teeming with challenges, strategic partnerships, and decisive leadership. It also reflects on the growth of NCDC, an exemplar national public health agency for the region.

This book stands not only as a testament to Chikwe and Vivianne's resilience and leadership but also as a blueprint for public health officials and leaders globally. It sheds light on the intricate decisions, the weight of leadership, and the importance of investing in public health infrastructure—offering invaluable insights and lessons for navigating crises in any corner of the world.

An Imperfect Storm is a beacon of hope in the darkness, sharing untold success stories from Africa. It not only sheds light on Nigeria's experience but also serves as an invaluable resource for understanding the decision-making processes during pandemics, accessible to a diverse audience—from scientists and public health professionals to students and the broader society. This book offers us a window into a world of hope and possibility—a world where competent leaders are empowered to lead. We are privileged to witness a story of transformation and hope within these pages, a story that demonstrates the potential of Africa when given the opportunity to shine.

I invite you to embark on this enlightening journey through "An Imperfect Storm" and hope that like I did, you will find a profound appreciation for the uncharted successes and potentials of the African continent. It is a reminder that even amidst the most challenging times, the hope for a brighter future continues to shine on our continent.

John Nkengasong
Former and Inaugural Director,
Africa Centres for Disease Control and Prevention

ALIGNMENT

Every decision we made in light of our changing circumstances evolved into the stars that perfectly aligned to form the narrative in An Imperfect Storm. Chikwe's appointment to head NCDC may not have been "on the cards," yet a convergence of events that started many years earlier, led to an important and transformative journey for us. Now, it appears as if those sequences of events were just waiting to unfold.

While writing this book, we reflected on how seemingly unconnected events and decisions we made along the way brought us back to Nigeria and Chikwe to NCDC. There was no five- or ten-year plan, we were always aligned in our desire to move back to Nigeria and contribute to its evolution and development. Little did we know at the time that this would be a once-in-a-lifetime experience (we hope).

If conventional wisdom had prevailed and the doomsday prediction had played out, this book would have been one of self-pity. However, when the COVID-19 pandemic struck, we confronted a perfect storm of challenges, including our health infrastructure, large and crowded urban areas and severe socioeconomic challenges. However, Nigeria emerged, demonstrating that we did not capitulate in our moment of dire straits.

However, at the onset of the outbreak, the fundamental elements of the response began to take shape, helped by decisions and choices made prior to the response, throughout the long process of establishing the country's public health institute, with its daily trials and tribulations.

It is now evident how incisive decision-making can shape one's destiny. Each decision we took over the years, influenced the trajectory not only of our lives together, but of the challenges we would face in the course of our lives. We first met on the university campus in Enugu, Nigeria. The stars (must have) aligned on that day, because although it felt like a chance meeting, it was meant to be.

The convergence of chance, decision, and circumstance were already in motion. Our lives have undergone many shifts over the years, none of which were planned with any precision. That is why this book is so important to us. It is a testament of many dreams, hopes, challenges and triumphs—for Chikwe and me as partners in love and life—but also of a nation in crisis.

Much has already been written about the COVID-19 response, but the common thread running throughout this story is that this experience was a test of resilience, and an opportunity for self-discovery and a reflection for ourselves and the country at large. The imperfect storm revealed hidden strengths and highlighted areas where we needed to strengthen our resolve. We discovered that some of the most profound lessons we learn in life, emerge when we are most challenged, and that resilience is built in the face of adversity.

Like many others, we found ourselves having to deal with the unpredictability of life, and it was in those moments of intense pressure and heightened vulnerability that we were able to uncover undiscovered aspects of ourselves. The unexpected turns and unchartered territory forced us to confront uncertainty and navigate through the turbulent transitions. Whether it is the upheaval of a family like many others during the pandemic or supporting Chikwe in his leadership role of the national public health institute, or simply being a citizen during a period of profound uncertainty.

We emerged from the storm a little changed, but stronger. The recollection of that imperfect storm became a testament to a chapter in our life when the stars aligned. It was never going to be plain sailing, but it was a test that reshaped and elevated our lives. Through the difficulty, we discovered a narrative that was distinctly ours, but also shared, woven with threads of resilience, growth, and optimism.

Vivianne

THE GATHERING

"Science knows no country, because knowledge belongs to humanity, and is the torch which illuminates the world."

Louis Pasteur

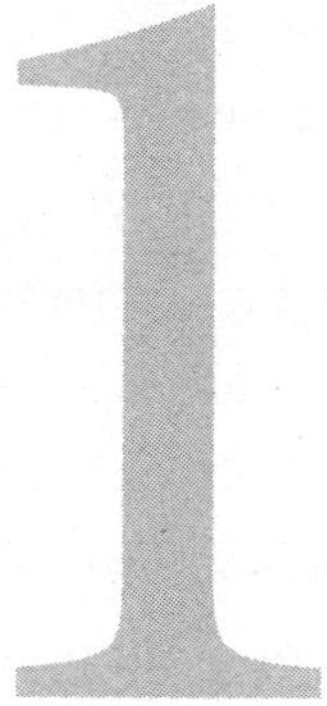

A CHRISTMAS BREAK

December 2019–January 2020

Time moved at a slower pace in the village. Days began with a leisurely breakfast—often fried yam and plantain with egg stew—shared by kin around a large dining table. Cousins, who had also returned to the village from different towns and cities across the country, joined us. Early visitors dropped by daily, seeking advice, offering gifts or simply looking to catch up, and we always made time to share a drink and a conversation. Life in the village at the end of the year was a time for reflection and reconnection with family. I cherished the mornings spent walking around our kindred, sitting with the *Umunna*, the older family members. We would engage in spirited debates about different things, trivial and weighty, even dialogues that stretched far beyond our vicinity. Our discussions were always peppered with Igbo proverbs, each trying to outdo the other in wit and wisdom.

December in Amaigbo, was more than just a time for celebrating Christmas. It was a time for discussing and solving family issues, celebrating births, mourning deaths, and reminiscing. It was a time for strengthening bonds and carrying on age-old traditions. The experience of sipping freshly tapped palm wine, surrounded by loved ones is indescribable. There was also the matter of lingering family disputes that were discussed with passion. Having everyone together was a great avenue to address and resolve grievances. Sadly, recent years have unfolded with economic hardships so people can hardly afford to travel home, but those who managed to make the journey always felt immensely rewarded. Every day was a new celebration, from traditional weddings to thanksgivings, to casual gatherings held in open spaces mysteriously livened by soft moonlight and Afrobeats music in the background.

When I was a child, my parents would take my siblings and me to the village every year at Christmas, and I now did the same for my family. Taking our family back to Amaigbo every year was a chance to pass on values that I had earlier learnt—the celebration of family, community, and tradition. I would watch our children form strong bonds with their cousins the same way I did in my childhood, allowing myself to be overwhelmed by nostalgia. Our children especially loved the freedom to roam from house to house in the village with their cousins. In those moments, I realised there was nowhere else we would rather be, even though time had brought along changes of its own.

Apart from the emergence of modern homes, there was greater connectivity to the 'outside world' than when I used to visit as a child. In the past, the village was a sanctuary, a place to escape the turmoil of urban life. Then came internet access, which revolutionised the dynamics of ruralness. There was no absolute on or off anymore. I couldn't entirely switch off and immerse myself in the village's beautiful serenity. However, the internet also made it easier to stay connected with friends and work no matter where we were. As the Director General of the Nigeria Centre for Disease Control (NCDC), it was especially important for me to correspond with my team and stay abreast of health emergencies within and beyond the country even when I was on leave. Unfortunately, viruses are little impolite things. They make no special consideration for holidays or other festivities. I dreaded being called by my Minister to enquire about an incident that I had not heard about, so being connected meant I was always on top of things.

The evening before everything changed, I was sitting on the veranda with some of our family members, as was our routine most evenings, enjoying each other's company over freshly tapped palm wine and an assortment of beer. The air was thick with dust from the *Okorosha* masquerade dance that had just taken place in the village square.

The next day was scorching. I collapsed onto the sofa in our sitting room, trying to catch my breath after a long morning walk-about. The whirring ceiling fan provided little relief from the sweltering heat. To distract myself, I mindlessly scrolled through my email and notifications. My scrolling finger stopped and hovered. There was a news report about a mysterious 'pneumonia-like' illness spreading in Wuhan, a town in China I had never heard of.

I hesitated for a moment, wondering if this was something significant or just another passing news story. There was already chatter among colleagues. I skimmed through the details and made a mental note to 'keep in view.' My experiences in dealing with infectious disease outbreaks had sharpened my intuition; the situation in Wuhan was one to keep an eye on. I have been involved, one way or another, in every major infectious disease outbreak since the 2000s—from the Severe Acute Respiratory Syndrome (SARS) epidemic caused by the virus SARS-CoV-1 in 2002–2004 to the 2009 H1N1 pandemic influenza and the 2014/15 Ebola outbreak in West

Africa. I quickly set up Google alerts and had a quick chat with the team at NCDC, advising them to keep close tabs on China. Nigeria's population is an estimated 200 million growing at an average rate of 3% per year. Add that to our largely tropical climate and difficult socio-economic indicators, and you have a perfect setting for the emergence and transmission of infectious diseases.

Given these circumstances, we couldn't afford the luxury of a 'December break' at NCDC. In fact, December was never an easy time, and we had to always be at our best to protect the health of our people. While most of the country shut down for the holidays, staff of NCDC often spent their Christmas working at our Emergency Operations Centres (EOCs), in the laboratory or across different states to support outbreak investigations. An identified team was always designated to work through the Christmas period and prepare against the increase in some infectious diseases that accompanied the New Year. For the average Nigerian, January heralded good tidings and new beginnings. For us at NCDC, January was more ominous. It would often arrive pregnant with a surge in Lassa fever cases. January was also the riskiest time for Meningococcal meningitis in the meningitis belt, which encompasses a chunk of northern Nigeria. In 2017, for example, we experienced a large meningitis outbreak (which started in December) caused by the meningitis C serogroup. It resulted in about 15,000 cases and led to nearly 2,000 deaths. This meant that despite being in the village, I had to remain accessible for constant calls from Commissioners for Health, State Epidemiologists, Chief Medical Directors, and other colleagues.

Vivianne and our two boys, Ginika and Barack, were used to my working all the time, but we still managed to find brief moments to unwind together. Every day while in the village, I would steal a couple of hours away from family time to review my emails and the various situation reports that were sent to me. I was afraid that something important would happen and I wouldn't know about it right away.

While combing through the latest news and social media updates, I noticed that some colleagues whom I knew and respected were discussing an alert from ProMED (Program for Monitoring Emerging Diseases), a public surveillance system I had been subscribed to for over 20 years. There it was again. The 'pneumonia of unknown cause' from Wuhan, China. It was a surreal feeling, watching the situation unfold as I sat in our home in Amaigbo. The world had changed so much since my early days as an epidemiologist, and the interconnectedness of our society meant that diseases could spread faster than ever before. While I hoped for the best, I had a disturbing feeling about this.

Days later, I found myself in a state of deep reflection. I thought about the last major infectious disease outbreak that caught national attention: the Ebola outbreak of 2014. The prevailing belief in its aftermath was that Nigeria hadn't only vanquished Ebola, but was also equipped to handle subsequent outbreaks. While we did prevent a large Ebola outbreak from happening in Nigeria, there was more to the success story. In the wake of our triumph, we lost the opportunity to reflect on aspects of our intervention that needed refinement and strengthen our capacity to respond to possible future outbreaks. One would think that our response to Ebola would have prompted the government to transform the country's national public health institute in Abuja into a world class agency; this didn't happen. By the time I was appointed in 2016, we were faced with the challenge of building an institution that had all the characteristics of a neglected orphan. This was three years before a pandemic that would change our lives forever.

I recall the calm before the storm—the first days of January 2020. A series of events led to the realisation that we were up against a force determined to ravage humanity.

January 1, 2020: I returned to Abuja. With better internet access, I sprung right into action, and I began by sifting through several reports from China. As a partner of the Global Outbreak Alert and Response Network (GOARN)[1], which is coordinated by the World Health Organization (WHO), NCDC has access to critical information about infectious disease outbreaks around the world.

January 2, 2020: We received more details about the cluster of pneumonia cases in China.

January 5, 2020: An alert from WHO came through the International Health Regulations IHR (2005) Event Information System for Member States. As the IHR National Focal Point for Nigeria, NCDC was responsible for sharing and receiving information relating to infectious diseases of international concern. Mrs Elsie Ilori, the Director of Surveillance at NCDC at the time—who was also the IHR lead—forwarded this information to me and the rest of the Management Team. My concern heightened. I worried that we might be facing a situation comparable to the 2002–2004 SARS outbreak, even though we had more tools at our disposal than we did during that outbreak.

During the SARS outbreak, I was a rookie epidemiologist at the Robert Koch Institute (RKI) in Berlin. The first SARS case was reported in March, prompting the national public health institute to begin identifying and quarantining contacts while following up on symptoms. Through the outbreak, Germany identified nine cases with no deaths. Ultimately, the global impact of the outbreak was 8,098 cases and 774 deaths across 6 continents.[2] Despite not being part of

---

1 GOARN is the Global Outbreak Alert and Response Network (GOARN). This is a network composed of numerous technical and public health institutions, laboratories, NGOs, and other organisations that work to observe and respond to threatening epidemics. GOARN works closely with and under the World Health Organization (WHO)

2 Summary of probable SARS cases with onset of illness from 1 November 2002 to 31 July 2003 https://www.who.int/publications/m/item/summary-of-probable-sars-cases-with-onset-of-illness-from-1-november-2002-to-31-july-2003

the growing SARS outbreak response team at the time, witnessing a major outbreak response up close and in real time marked the beginning of a phenomenal learning curve. The SARS outbreak changed the global perception of the risks associated with emerging infectious diseases and inspired many countries to re-engage with epidemic preparedness.

January 9, 2020: WHO reported that Chinese authorities had determined the cause of the Wuhan outbreak—a new coronavirus. It was time to act. I pulled together a small team at NCDC. The first time we convened, I could sense the tension in the atmosphere as I laid out my expectations. The mandate was simple: all eyes on Wuhan. This small team was led by one of our very best field epidemiologists at NCDC, Dr Olaolu Aderinola. Olaolu and his team worked tirelessly, sifting through countless reports and guidelines from WHO and other organisations, distilling the most crucial information into concise and digestible reports.

January 10, 2020: Tension and pressure mounted as the outbreak continued to spread in China. We had to ramp up our approach, and I began providing regular written and verbal reports to the Honourable Minister of Health, Dr Osagie Ehanire, and the Minister of State for Health, Dr Adeleke Mamora. It was alarming that even this preliminary stage wasn't smooth sailing. For a long time, I tried to convince the Minister of Health to prioritise health security, but he had been resistant. He didn't see the need to allocate funds specifically for health emergencies, arguing that donors and partners were already supporting NCDC. Specifically, he had objected to the inclusion of health security as part of the 5% devoted to health emergencies in the Basic Health Care Provision Fund (BHCPF) despite my best efforts to explain the risks. We were better prepared than we were during the Ebola outbreak in 2014, but still had a long road to walk. I made it my mission to persuade the Minister to re-evaluate his position on health security.

The BHCPF, a crucial funding mechanism for healthcare in Nigeria, is funded with 1% of the consolidated revenue of the Federal Government of Nigeria. It was established by the 2014 National Health Act to provide additional financial support to the routine government budget allocation for health, ensuring that essential health services are available and affordable to all Nigerians, particularly those in vulnerable or underserved communities. This funding is critical for strengthening the healthcare system, and as we often advocated for, it was necessary to ensure that Nigeria was better prepared for health emergencies like the COVID-19 pandemic.

January 14, 2020: WHO confirmed 41 global cases. Port Health Services had increased screening at Nigerian airports—checking for spiked temperatures and visitors with a travel history to China. Media outlets continued to endlessly speculate about the impending possibility of the virus crossing into the country. Nigeria was already operating in a context where there was not a lot of trust in government institutions, and the apprehension of doom and gloom was emerging.

January 15, 2020: We provided our first report on the novel coronavirus during the weekly Federal Executive Council (FEC) meeting which was chaired by His Excellency, President Muhammadu Buhari. It was a testament to the team's hard work, but it wasn't our first report to FEC. We had been providing weekly infectious disease outbreak reports for nearly three years, at the request of the previous Minister of Health, Professor Isaac Adewole.

These reports had focused on epidemic prone diseases such as Lassa fever, cholera, and measles, which were considered important due to their potential to disrupt not just health, but also the economy and social stability. With this experience, I was grateful for the opportunity to present on the novel coronavirus at such a critical time. WHO had conducted a threat assessment which placed China at high risk of spread, other countries in Asia at moderate risk, and countries outside Asia—including Nigeria—at a low risk. This assessment was based on the limited information available to WHO at the time. Despite this low risk, we knew what needed to be done. We needed to protect our people, but when public health is addressed from a political standpoint, a lot of things will not go as planned, and visions will collide.

The interplay between politics and public health has always piqued my curiosity. How do our political leaders use the information in the regular infectious disease outbreak reports provided by NCDC? Did they understand the potential catastrophic impact of an outbreak? The Ebola outbreak was meant to be a wake-up call that exposed our vulnerability to emerging diseases, but did the political leaders deduce how desperately we needed to improve public health and healthcare delivery in Nigeria?

As news of the outbreak in Wuhan intensified, we had to amplify our approach. This meant capturing the attention of Nigerians. I made frequent appearances in media interviews to raise awareness and promote preparedness measures. Meanwhile, our small monitoring team had quickly evolved into the National Coronavirus Preparedness Group (NCPG). At the time, NCDC had a total of 300 staff members, with 100 of them recently recruited and undergoing orientation. To put this into perspective, our counterparts at the US Centers for Disease Control had over 50,000 staff members while the UK Health Security Agency (Public Health England—PHE at the time) had about 5,500 staff members in England alone. Most of our staff members were already deployed in response to the increasing number of Lassa fever cases which required constant attention. While we couldn't redeploy people out of the Lassa fever EOC, we couldn't ignore the threat of the coronavirus outbreak either. I started holding meetings late into the night with a small team of colleagues, brainstorming options and scenarios and taking notes in my notebook that I carried with me everywhere.

As we had done in the past with other major infectious disease outbreaks, we reached out to our partners and invited them to join us in the preparedness group. The team included colleagues from the Port Health team of the Federal Ministry of Health, WHO, US CDC, PHE, UNICEF, and other organisations that always worked closely with NCDC. We enlisted residents and graduates of the Nigeria Field Epidemiology and Laboratory Training Programme (NFELTP) who were dispersed across various Ministries and agencies throughout the country. These graduates were some of our most valuable assets, as they were always available to provide support for outbreak response. Together with our partners, we created a formidable team ready to tackle the challenges of the coronavirus outbreak in Nigeria.

We reviewed our National Pandemic Influenza Preparedness and Response Plan which had been developed after the H1N1 pandemic in 2009. For the first time ever, we were considering the worst-case-scenario and examining our own capacity to manage laboratory, surveillance, risk communications, and supply chain needs. On a national level, we had developed a lot of the anticipated capacity, but the state levels still had several weak links in the chain. With outbreaks, weak links provide the perfect environment for devastating consequences. We decided that one of the most urgent things to do was assess the required capacities across states and make immediate plans to support them. In a meeting with WHO Country Office, my primary request to the Country Representative was for the WHO team to work with us in reviewing our preparedness at the state level. The results were sobering, for example, we had fewer than 300 functional intensive care beds in the public sector, to serve the entire country.

We set out immediate goals for improvement. Our initial objectives were to ensure that every state had at least one EOC and one functional molecular laboratory as well as a digital surveillance system. We already knew which states had molecular laboratories and

EOCs, but needed to ensure that these facilities were fully equipped and staffed to respond to a potential outbreak. Progress was slow, and limited funding was a major challenge.

The one area that I was most concerned about was our capacity to provide clinical care. Apart from the Infectious Disease Hospital in Yaba, Irrua Specialist Teaching Hospital (ISTH) in Edo State; Federal Medical Centre, Owo in Ondo State; the Alex Ekwueme Federal Teaching Hospital, Abakaliki, in Ebonyi State—and other health facilities in our Lassa fever network—I wasn't confident in our capacity for infectious disease management in other hospitals across the country. The detection of cases at ports of entry was largely the responsibility of the Port Health Services unit of the Federal Ministry of Health, one of the most under-resourced units in the entire ministry. The ministry itself wasn't famous for its operational efficiency, and not all its departments were open to working with NCDC or collaborating with our nascent agency nor were they used to the agile way we worked. We forged on regardless. Our preparedness group conducted risk assessments and inventory of needs across the country.

As days went by, we received more reports of confirmed cases in Wuhan. The news cycle was filled with 24-hour coverage of health workers donning full personal protective equipment (PPE) and struggling to cope in China. We were bombarded with rumours of health workers in China being restricted from speaking to the media, and we saw graphic images of the wet market in Wuhan, the suspected 'ground-zero' of the virus' origin. The thought of having to mount such a response if faced with a similar scenario left us feeling extremely anxious.

By the time China finished building a 1,500-room hospital within five days, a feat broadcast live around the world, the plot had thickened. It became undeniable that we were confronted with a major threat with the risk of spreading globally. Our risk assessments showed that the situation had rapidly evolved, with clusters of cases being reported in countries across the world. Many people wondered how African countries would cope, given our fragile healthcare systems. The assumption was always that countries in Africa would suffer the severest outcomes.

January 21, 2020: I sent the Honourable Minister of Health the first version of a public health advisory that NCDC was issuing to all Nigerians, advising them of the risks, our assessment of it, and advice on what they needed to do should they feel unwell. I provided the Minister of Health with regular reports and updates—often sent daily. In addition to these updates, we used social media and regular appearances on television and radio to share what we knew about the new infectious disease outbreak in China and its potential implication for Nigeria. We knew that timely and effective communication was crucial in the face of a potential outbreak, especially in a country where trust in the public sector was already low.

January 22, 2020: Our first public health advisory was published. This was the first step to alerting Nigerians, warning them of the risk of spread while trying not to arouse panic. We battled misinformation and rumours as the situation evolved by maintaining clear and continuous communication with the public. In the coming months, our commitment to timely and transparent communication would become even more critical in the fight against COVID-19.

2

AVANT LE DELUGE

August 2016

In early 2016, a long-term Nigerian friend and colleague with whom I had worked closely in the UK, asked a question that caught me off guard. He asked, "If you were offered a position as head of the Nigeria Centre for Disease Control, would you take it?"

Without much thought, I replied, "If it were to become available, I would be interested."

Months later, I had just returned to Johannesburg—where I was living with my family at the time—from the 2016 International Aids Conference that held in Durban. It was just another morning, and Vivianne had left to drop our children off at school, where they had early starts and then to work. I was still in my pyjamas, sipping my coffee and getting ready for the day when the phone rang. It was a friend from Abuja who sounded unusually giddy with excitement.

He told me that the President had just removed all the existing heads of the health sector parastatals. I wasn't exactly sure how this information concerned me until he dropped the bomb: "You have been appointed to lead the Nigeria Centre for Disease Control as its Chief Executive Officer."

Effective Immediately. Really? No advance warning, no letter of appointment, just an instruction. The words reverberated through my mind. *You have been appointed . . . Nigeria Centre for Disease Control . . . Chief . . . Executive . . . Officer . . .*

Not that I doubted myself, but this was happening too suddenly and appeared to be completely out of the blue. But was it? My mind rushed back to the conversation with my friend in the UK and my response to his very unsuspecting question.

If it were to become available, I would be interested.

There it was. I had given my consent without realising. Then it struck me. Vivianne wasn't aware of the first call, nor this job offer, and now it was already in the news. I wondered how she would receive the news.

When Vivianne got home that evening, I told her that we needed to have an urgent conversation, while assuring her that there was no problem. Once she was seated, I cut to the chase.

"I'm being offered a job in Nigeria."

The look on her face was priceless, and I could tell that she wasn't quite sure what to say. She was still processing the news. The continuous ringing of my phone jarred the silence.

"Your name was on the radio this morning. You have been appointed Director of NCDC!" the voice blared from the speaker, almost a shriek. It was a friend from Nigeria. I stared at Vivianne, and she held my gaze as we both tried to make sense of our shared uncertainty.

Later that day, the President's spokesperson formally announced that I had been appointed to lead NCDC with immediate effect. The media in Nigeria was buzzing with the news. It was a surreal moment, but I knew deep down that this was an opportunity I couldn't turn down. This was an opportunity to make a real difference in our country. And even though the prospect of giving up the comfort and stability of our life in Johannesburg was daunting, I was ready to take the plunge. After all, the call to serve one's country was a once-in-a-lifetime event. But to say that I felt overwhelmed in that moment would be a gross understatement.

Everyone had an opinion on what I should do next. My loved ones spoke with conviction about the important work that lay ahead, and in true Nigerian fashion, offered their unwavering support.

As news of my appointment spread, I received a deluge of offers from well-meaning individuals who were eager to assist me in navigating the complex Nigerian system. It was a humbling experience, and I was grateful for their generosity. Still, I understood that making a real difference in the lives of Nigerians was my ultimate responsibility. I knew the agency I was invited to lead was at a liminal stage of its evolution, and I was expected to chart the next steps for NCDC.

The agency's journey began in 2007 when the 51st National Council on Health—the highest decision-making body on health in Nigeria—endorsed its establishment. It took four more years and a new government before the first formal steps were taken to fully create it. In 2011, the agency's nucleus was formed from various units in the Federal Ministry of Health, including the Epidemiology Division, the Avian Influenza Project, and the Nigeria Field Epidemiology and Laboratory Training Programme (NFELTP). This was done through a memo signed by the then Permanent Secretary of the Ministry of Health, Mr Linus Awute. While most staff members transitioned to the new parastatal, some chose to stay in the Ministry, resisting the change.

Fortunately, a grant from the US CDC provided five consultants to support the initial staff that migrated to NCDC from the Ministry of Health. The agency started its operations from the offices of the Nigeria Field Epidemiology Training Programme in Asokoro, Abuja, which was funded by the US Government. After enduring the challenges associated with sharing offices, NCDC finally received a building in the Jabi area of Abuja from the Ministry of Health. This marked the beginning of the agency's journey to fulfil its mandate of leading the preparedness, detection, and response to infectious disease outbreaks and public health emergencies in Nigeria. Despite limited funding, the agency remained steadfast in its mission, determined to make a positive impact on the country's public health landscape.

My decision to take up the new position in Nigeria wasn't just professional; it was a personal decision that would significantly impact our family. We would have to leave the life we had built in South Africa and start anew in Nigeria. Vivianne already had to endure numerous unexpected twists and turns in our journey together, so this was just another chapter in the story of our lives. Despite the upheaval, I was comforted by her encouragement. She was always by my side, ready to tackle whatever challenges came our way.

Vivianne sprang into action, preparing for our move back to Nigeria. In the face of uncertainty, having a formidable partner can make all the difference. Her resolution was all the motivation I needed to seal the deal, assuming the position of Chief Executive Officer of NCDC in August 2016.

From the outset, there was pressure to succeed. The President's surprise announcement ushered in new leadership for all five major health sector parastatals including the National Primary Health Care Development Agency (NPHCDA); National Agency for the Control of AIDS (NACA); Nigerian Institute of Medical Research (NIMR);

and the National Health Insurance Scheme (NHIS). The popular narrative was that the complete overhaul in leadership was much needed to drive innovation in the health sector.

In my usual collaborative nature, I sought acquaintanceship with other newly appointed heads of the health parastatal. We bonded over our shared visions to provide the trustworthy leadership the health sector needed, agreeing to work together to achieve this. We understood that our work would be crucial in shaping the future of public health in Nigeria. What I didn't realise, however, was the extent of uncertainty tainting this new horizon stretched before me. A mere three years later, we were met with a challenge we couldn't have ever foreseen.

Figure 1: The five new Chief Executive Officers of health sector parastatals, from left to right, Professor Usman Yusuf (NHIS), Professor Babatunde Salako (NIMR), Dr Faisal Shuaib (NPHCDA), Dr Sani Aliyu (NACA) and me.

3

AN UNFOLDING PANDEMIC

January 2020

By the end of January, it had become clear to the global community that we were dealing with a large infectious disease outbreak. China had reported the identification of a new type of coronavirus, initially known as 2019-nCoV. Beyond Wuhan, where the first cluster of cases had emerged, other provinces in China had begun to report sporadic cases.

I fed my adrenaline surge with every piece of information I could find. At the early stage, the epidemiology of the pathogen wasn't yet fully understood, and the mode of transmission was still unclear, but more knowledge about the virus was emerging. There was emerging evidence of human-to-human transmission, with numerous cases reported among healthcare workers. This crucial bit of knowledge would change all the assumptions about the outbreak. Various emerging models predicted a doomsday scenario for most of the world, particularly for African countries. Pressure was mounting as many global health professionals began to call for the declaration of a Public Health Emergency of International Concern (PHEIC).

The concept of a 'PHEIC' originated in 2005, when WHO revised the International Health Regulations (IHR) as a framework for the global community to respond to health emergencies. It was a recognition that the spread of infectious diseases had become a global threat, requiring a coordinated response from WHO's member states and the world. Prior to the COVID-19 pandemic, a PHEIC had been declared five times—including for the 2009 H1N1 influenza outbreak; twice in 2014, following the resurgence of polio in Afghanistan, Pakistan, and Nigeria, and during the West African Ebola outbreak, Zika virus disease in 2016 and the Kivu Ebola epidemic in 2018.This time, the journey to declaring the outbreak a PHEIC wasn't without controversies.

I received an invitation to join the important WHO Emergency Committee on the outbreak, one of the prerequisite steps to declare a PHEIC. This committee was tasked by the International Health Regulations (IHR) to advise the Director General (DG) of WHO on whether a PHIEC was necessary for this particular event, considering all the evidence available at the time. The committee was comprised of experienced virologists, epidemiologists, and public-health experts from around the world, each selected for their individual expertise, not institutional affiliation.

During the first meeting held by teleconference on January 22 and 23, there was no consensus by the Emergency Committee on whether a PHEIC should be declared at this time. It was a heated debate, with each member presenting their own arguments and perspectives. Despite the disagreements, we all shared the same sense of urgency and responsibility to protect public health. The pressure was immense, and we knew that any recommendation we made would have far-reaching consequences. Although the views varied, everyone tried to reach the best possible conclusion based on the information at hand. The Emergency Committee had divergent views on whether the event constituted a PHEIC or not and concluded that the event did not constitute a PHEIC at the time, and proposed to be reconvened in a matter of days to examine the situation further.

With emerging information on the spread, the second WHO Emergency Committee meeting was convened on January 30. There were so many factors to consider, such as the speed of spread of the virus, especially as the mode of transmission wasn't as clear as we would have wished for, neither did the committee have much access to data on the clinical severity of cases or the risk of death.

A consensus was however reached to advise the WHO DG to declare the outbreak a PHEIC. The DG accepted the recommendations of the emergency committee and later that day, the announcement was made.

The delay between the two meetings of the emergency committee was one week. One week was indeed a potentially long time for a pathogen to spread further, and a lot has been made of this apparent delay in hindsight. But it is also necessary to understand the information requirements on the many other factors that influence such decisions and the burden on committee members to draw the best conclusions from the available information. However, here lies the crucial question: would the trajectory of the pandemic have been significantly altered if the declaration of the PHEIC had come a week earlier? I think most scientists would conclude that this wouldn't have been the case. This debate is understandable, considering the volatility at the intersection of science, public health, and how it affects our perception of risk. Nonetheless, these conversations linger. Conversations about whether the declaration of a PHEIC could have been made sooner, with some countries demanding a review of the declaration processes. The thresholds for the declaration have been a subject of intense debate. Amidst these speculations, the world quaked at the mercy of a rapidly spreading virus and innumerable unknowns. WHO and the Emergency Committee did their best to balance the need for caution with the need to act quickly to contain the outbreak.

Anxiously, I watched the DG of WHO declare the outbreak a PHEIC on January 30, 2020. There were 7,818 infections confirmed. By the declaration, WHO was empowered to provide more international support to countries in need and make recommendations to slow and contain the spread of the virus. Countries were beginning to implement their own travel restrictions, primarily focused on flights from China and further expanding to other countries with 'ongoing transmission' of 2019-nCoV. At this nascent stage of the pandemic, it became clear that expediting research on the new virus, its transmissibility and virulence as well as the public health response was critical to curb its spread. The urgency of the situation was palpable, and the global community was galvanised into a quest for answers.

In the first week of February, I received an invitation to a meeting in Geneva convened by WHO. It was an opportunity for scientists and public health experts from around the world to share their insights on the outbreak. When I arrived at the meeting, I was immediately taken by the sense of determination and focus in the room. Everyone seemed awfully aware that the clock was ticking, and time was of the essence. We also learnt more details on China's lockdown of Wuhan province in an effort to contain the outbreak. A handful of cases had already been reported outside China, including in Europe and the United States. There was a significant focus on cruise ships, as they seemed especially susceptible at the time to being super-spreaders of the COVID-19 virus.

During my time in Geneva, I had the privilege of chairing a tension-filled plenary session with my colleague, Nisia Trindade

Lima who led Brazil's national public health agency, the Oswaldo Cruz Foundation (Fiocruz). We discussed the roles of national public health agencies in leading the response to the emergence of infectious diseases. I also had the opportunity to connect with my colleagues—Ahmed Ogwell and Raji Tajudeen from the Africa Centres for Disease Control and Prevention. We discussed the potential opportunities for strengthening emergency response capacity in the African region, but we also acknowledged the immense expectations placed on this young institution; the Africa CDC which had only been launched in 2017. But even as the pandemic was unfolding, our agencies were already collaborating.

Figure 2: Chairing the Research Forum on novel corona virus 2019 with Dr Nisia Trindade Lima.

From the beginning of January, I had pushed my colleagues to their limit, bombarding them with WhatsApp messages whenever I had a new idea. We knew that our existing response capacity was focused mainly on Lagos and Abuja, with only a few other states experienced in managing severe infectious disease, especially Lassa fever cases. Thankfully, we received early support from WHO to establish testing capacity at NCDC National Reference Laboratory (NRL), but we still didn't have the reagents for testing. We leveraged our existing collaboration with the national public health agency in Germany, RKI. Coincidentally, a few colleagues from RKI were coming to Nigeria for a joint ProMED-RKI-NCDC training activity. ProMed was engaging its first 'editors' for Nigeria/Africa, and NCDC had offered to host this training on our campus.

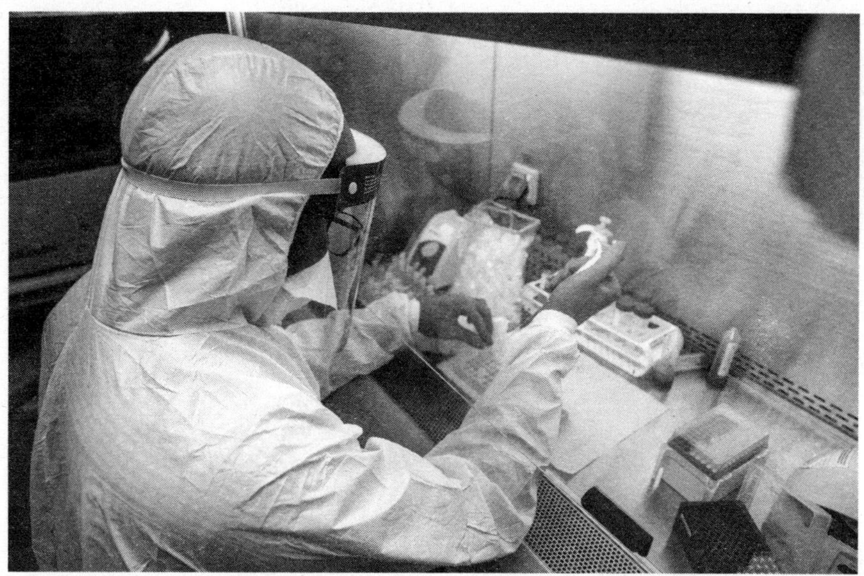

Figure 3: A colleague working in the National Reference Laboratory.

When we heard that our colleagues in Germany had developed the first diagnostic test for the coronavirus recommended by WHO, we asked if they could bring a few test kits to Nigeria. The President of RKI and a long-term friend, Professor Lothar Wieler, kindly agreed to our request, despite the local pressure. The RKI team arrived in Abuja on January 20, but unfortunately realised that they had brought the wrong box from Berlin. Despite the disappointment which we all felt, we didn't give up. Thankfully, global logistics systems were still active at the time. Within days, through DHL's service and the dedicated work of our RKI colleagues, our first diagnostic test kits arrived in Abuja on January 27. It was one of the first of many instances where NCDC's partnerships around the world would serve Nigeria throughout the pandemic.

With support from Africa CDC and WHO, we organised an intensive training for staff of NCDC. They were equipped with technical knowledge of laboratory testing, risk communications, and infection prevention control (IPC) for the new disease by now renamed COVID-19. Whenever we were asked to send one person to represent Nigeria, I always pushed back and requested more. Training only one person for a country like Nigeria—the same offer made to our much smaller West African neighbours—was akin to a drop in the ocean. We negotiated for the training of at least two colleagues in each area and began a 'step-down training' immediately after they returned. Each person selected for these training opportunities had the responsibility of training other colleagues at national and state levels.

The true strengths of multilateralism and global collaboration were evident in our preparedness for the coronavirus outbreak in Nigeria. The support we received from WHO, Africa CDC and RKI at the early response stages were important catalysts as we prepared for our first case. By participating in global decision making, we contributed to policy and research, learnt from other countries' experiences, and targeted our focus where it was most needed.

This wasn't just about Nigeria. A bigger picture was at play, featuring global solidarity in the face of a pandemic that would know no borders.

A CALLING

1980–2016

I owe whatever I've become to the tree from which I fell.

My parents, Umelobi and Edith Ihekweazu, played an inextricable role in shaping my interests and character as I grew up. Their courtship began at the University of Hamburg, Germany amid protests against the devastating impact of the Nigerian civil war. The era of social activism at the time must have been partly fuelled by the vivid images of the war on television, which highlighted incredible hardships inflicted by the conflict on civilian populations. It was the first major conflict that played out so vividly on TV screens around the world.

Being Nigerian, my father was part of the protests on campus for obvious reasons, but my German mother's motivation, I suspect, was driven by the pain of being a post-war child herself. She was born in 1941, at the beginning of the Second World War, and the circumstances of her childhood were far from the prosperity that is found in Germany today. My parents fell in love and married shortly after the war ended, setting up home in Hamburg, where my sister, Ada, and I were born.

We relocated to Nigeria when I was about three years old, mainly because my parents wanted to help with post-war rebuilding. The post-war period in South-eastern Nigeria was serene and calm, but it was also a period of scarcity and lack. Nonetheless, they both found work at the University of Nigeria, Nsukka (UNN). My mother started as a lecturer in the Department of Foreign Languages, while my father was one of three doctors at the university hospital. Our home was a standard bungalow on campus, but what set it apart was that every room had a bookshelf adorned with a rich variety of books. My mother, an ardent reader by virtue of work and leisure, instilled the love for reading in my sister and me from an early age. My childhood in the small university town of Nsukka was a truly unique experience. Subsequently, our family expanded with the birth of my brother, Edozie.

As a young boy, I was fortunate to be surrounded by some of the brightest minds in Nigeria. On many occasions, my parents would host social gatherings with their colleagues and friends from the university community. Our sparsely furnished sitting room often accommodated the likes of Chinua Achebe, Emmanuel Obiechina, Anya O. Anya, Obiora Udechukwu, the Dikes, the Mmaduewesis, and other famous Nigerian writers and academics. To me, they were regular people, but I was always fascinated by their animated conversations about Africa's progress and challenges. I would sit at the dining table, pretending to be reading while soaking in their conversations. I heard names like Nyerere, Nkrumah and Lumumba with very little understanding of their place in history. I knew that my mother, was fascinated by the work of Frantz Fanon, but I was too young to understand why.

The fusion of ideas and opinions resulting from eavesdropping on the musings of great minds sowed seeds of intellectual curiosity that would accompany me for a lifetime. I realised the importance and joy of engaging in meaningful conversations, of exchanging ideas from a place of humility and deepened awareness. These experiences would shape my thinking and influence my approach to problem-solving for years to come.

Our family's campus home was a hub of activity. We would often wake to the shrill cry of an ambulance picking my father to oversee an emergency at the university medical centre where he worked. Home was more or less a subsidiary outpatient clinic as he would receive patients there beyond work hours—mostly colleagues and their children. In fact, a small storage room in our house was converted into a mini pharmacy stocked with medicines. My father's dedication to the community was remarkable, and he was highly respected for it.

There was a palpable sense of pride and warmth in being the child of the university doctor. People would give us lifts on the way home or recognise me as *nwa* doc—child of the doctor. Seeing my father with a stethoscope around his neck as he headed to work defined my childhood. The respect and recognition my father garnered from the community inspired me to be like him, to study medicine and become a doctor. I wanted to impact people's lives the way he did.

My mother was a trailblazer in her own field, breaking barriers and becoming the first female professor at the University of Nigeria, Nsukka. She was a woman of remarkable persistence and unwavering dedication, and her tireless efforts in the face of challenging circumstances left a lasting impression on my siblings and me. Besides her work, she was deeply involved in the Children's Centre Library as well as the University Women's Association. She encouraged us to read widely and explore our interests, fostering a deep sense of curiosity and love for learning (there wasn't much else to do other than read and play anyway; we didn't have a functioning television at home for most of my childhood). Her typewriter could be heard every evening echoing through the stillness of the night as she typed her manuscripts.

In 1983, at the age of 12, I was accepted into the Federal Government College, Enugu (FGCE)—my first time away from family. Boarding school life was tough, especially during the first year; I had more sad than happy days. While I enjoyed attending classes and expanding my knowledge, the hours between the end of lessons and supper were particularly difficult. The older boys in the dormitories would often take advantage of younger students like me, forcing us to run endless errands such as fetching water for their baths, buying bread at the tuck shop, or doing their laundry. If we were found in the hostels on afternoons, it meant a never-ending stream of errands and chores. I spent many afternoons with my classmates, wandering the sports fields in exhausted boredom to pass time and steer clear of the older boys. Today, I'm grateful for the friendships that were built from this challenging situation. They sustained me through boarding school and thereafter.

In 1989, I sat for the national exams that would determine which university I would attend and was pleased to gain admission into the University of Nigeria to study medicine. This was the culmination of years of hard work and dedication, and I was determined to make the most of this opportunity to learn and grow. My first year at medical school was a time of exploration and fun. Instead of burying myself in textbooks, I found myself basking in the campus social scene, enjoying every moment of it. I occasionally had access to my parent's vehicle, given that we lived on campus, and I relished the social capital it afforded me.

During the summer vacation before my second year, I travelled to Germany to be with my mother who was on a research trip. While I stayed behind in Germany to spend more time with my grandmother, my mother headed back home to Nigeria. On her way to Nsukka, she was involved in a head-on collision with a trailer that was overtaking a vehicle.

She didn't survive the accident.

My sister Ada, who was also in the car, survived the crash but was admitted to the hospital and spent some time in intensive care.

My mother died at the prime of her career and at the brink of my adulthood. Edozie was just 15 years old when we lost her. Every day seemed tumultuous thereafter. I felt lost, heartbroken—I felt many emotions that, thinking back, I cannot coherently explain. Her death left a void in our family that could never be filled. She was our rock, the one who held us together and taught us valuable lessons about compassion, kindness, and generosity. My father was devastated, but he knew that he had to be strong for his children. He put on a brave face and pushed through the difficult funeral arrangements, suddenly finding himself in a new dual role as father and mother.

As much as I wanted it to, life didn't stop after my mother's passing. After the funeral, I had to soldier on with my studies. The toughest period of medical school was just ahead. At the end of our third year, we had to take the second Bachelor of Medicine, Bachelor of Surgery medical student's exams, referred to as second MB. This exam was a make-or-break test that determined whether a student would progress into their fourth year. Unlike all other exams at the medical school, which allowed students multiple re-sits, second MB provided only one chance to retake it.

Each year, one out of four medical students did not make it beyond this exam, leading to the end of their medical school journey. I was determined to be at the better end of this statistic.

After long hours of overwhelming hard work, I sailed through. I passed the second MB on my first attempt, proceeding to my fourth year of medical school during which I began my clinical training. Every day, we would take a bus from our campus to the hospital, donning our white coats with stethoscopes around our necks. It felt like we were finally doing what we came for. However, we soon discovered that real-life diseases didn't always present in the same way as they appeared in textbooks. We had to rely on softer skills not taught in class—like communication, touch, and intuition—to help us arrive at the most likely diagnosis.

During my final year, I met the woman who would become my wife. Vivianne was visiting her older sister Christine, from the UK. We hit it off immediately, going on several dates in Enugu. I was captivated by her composure and quiet confidence. She had a keen sense of purpose and a thirst for knowledge that I found incredibly attractive. We quickly became friends, spending as much time as we could before Vivianne returned to London to continue her studies. Despite the distance between us, we stayed in touch, unsure of what the future held but hopeful that our strong connection would endure.

After medical school, I was fairly certain about my future aspirations and what I wanted to specialise in. Inspired by one of our charismatic lecturers—Professor Aghaji, a cardio-thoracic surgeon at our teaching hospital—I set my sights on becoming a surgeon. He had a larger-than-life personality that was impossible to miss in the hospital. His deep baritone and towering presence commanded respect from all who interacted with him. He had a legendary status, not just because he was the only person at the hospital at the time who could perform open heart surgery, but also due to his intervention on many apparently hopeless cases. The more I observed him in action, the more I knew surgery was the field for me. Something about the intricateness of the human body and the precision required to make someone whole again called to me. I was determined to follow in Professor Aghaji's footsteps and become a surgeon.

I finally completed my medical degree in 1996, one year later than planned due to unforeseen strike actions and delays. The entire 'Class of 95' actually graduated in 1996, a reality of tertiary education in Nigeria. I was eager to begin my career and started my housemanship in Aba, a town in southeastern Nigeria. While most of my colleagues opted to stay in larger cities or places near their alma mater, I chose to take on the challenge of a less popular location. Not competing for patients with other doctors meant that I had more opportunities to learn and gain valuable practical experience. On the other hand, the nurses demanded competence, and the senior doctors weren't only unapproachable but often completely unavailable. I found that I had to think on my feet and learn quickly to survive in the fast-paced world of medicine.

I recall assisting women during childbirth with the aid of battery-powered torches due to infrequent power supply. It was always a surreal experience, but our teamwork and resourcefulness enabled us to safely deliver the babies and provide the necessary care for the mothers most of the time. Likewise, there was a satisfaction that came with seeing desperately ill children recover in the paediatric ward. These children often arrived in critical situations, weak and unresponsive due to malaria or dehydration. I spent as much time as I could in the paediatric ward, soaking up the positive energy and the joy of seeing these children regain their health.

After spending my housemanship year in Aba, I was posted to a clinic in Lagos for my National Youth Service—the compulsory one-year service scheme for graduates of higher institutions, started post-civil war for nation-building and promoting national unity. The clinic was situated in the heart of a sprawling Police College in Lagos State, serving an overpopulated and struggling community. Many of the family systems were fragile, with single mothers raising multiple children on their own. It was a completely different community set up from Aba. My role as a doctor went beyond just diagnosing and treating illnesses. I found myself giving significant counselling, listening to the problems of police officers and their families, providing comfort, and offering practical advice. The clinic often ran out of essential medicines, leaving me with no other option but to use my own limited resources to buy medicines for these families.

Meanwhile, I continued to nurture my dream of becoming a surgeon. I hoped to specialise in the US. However, to get into a surgical training programme there, I had to pass the three stages of the US Medical Licensing Exam (USMLE) which would take about 18 months to complete. The thought of a year and a half studying for exams didn't appeal to me, so I decided to pursue a Master's degree in Public Health at Heinrich Heine University in Düsseldorf, Germany as a stop-gap measure, planning to take the exams in parallel.

My learning experience in Germany was transformative and different from that in Nigeria. At Heinrich Heine University, they prioritised critical thinking and encouraged an open learning environment where students could be boldly expressive. To my greatest surprise, I became increasingly drawn to the complexities of public health issues as I delved deeper into my studies. For example, I deeply enjoyed the debates about broad health policy. I loved the fact that there were no right or wrong answers, and every problem had to be approached with a nuanced understanding of context and culture. Eventually, public health stole my heart. I became so immersed in it that I kept postponing my final USMLE exams and eventually became comfortable with de-prioritising my dreams of specialising in the US.

Everything changed when I realised that public health was my truest calling.

At the end of my masters' programme in 2000, I was hired as a scientific officer at the Robert Koch Institute (RKI) in Berlin, Germany's national public health agency. I was determined to deepen my knowledge of how infectious diseases emerged and spread. At the time, I was working on a project on hospital acquired infections and while it seemed practical, it was a slow burn and difficult area.

My keen interest in the fast-moving world of emerging infectious disease threats led me to discover the European Programme for Field Epidemiology Training (EPIET), a two-year training programme that prepares public health experts in competencies for intervention epidemiology (often also referred to as field epidemiology). Fellows were usually trained in national or regional centres on the surveillance and control of infectious diseases. The aim of EPIET was to provide public health specialists with specific field epidemiology expertise to work in countries within the European Union. Those selected to undertake this training would be required to gain direct experience in public health institutes in any European country. A senior mentor delivers the majority of the training, with minimal, but targeted traditional classroom teaching. The aim was for the field epidemiologist to gain hands-on practical experience in surveillance and outbreak response. It felt like the perfect programme for me, and I worked hard on the application and interviews. Despite getting close to my goal getting into the programme, I wasn't selected and was deeply disappointed.

I was lucky to reconnect with Vivianne, who had graduated and was working in London. In the absence of mobile phones and easy access to the internet, our relationship had drifted. This time around, I was more determined to make it work. As our friendship blossomed, I began making regular trips to London to see her. Later in 2003, I left my job at RKI and moved to London where Vivianne was living and working. We got married on a hot summer day in London and had a large, bootstrapped wedding with loads of family and friends. We were happy and settled into married life and the hustle of life in London.

I quickly found work as a public health analyst with the UK's National Health Service at the Haringey Primary Care Trust. Seeing how public health worked at the local level in the UK was eye-opening, but I couldn't shake the feeling that I needed more direct experience in field epidemiology. So, I decided to apply for the EPIET programme once again. This time, I was delighted to be accepted. I was finally going to get my chance to gain the practical experience I craved and help make a difference in the world of infectious disease control.

Through the EPIET programme, I was assigned to work with England's public health agency, then known as the Health Protection Agency (HPA), the second national public health agency of my career at the time. Although I was accepted into the training programme in the UK, instead of being posted to London—which was much sought after—I was posted to the Southwest of England's regional office, based in the small Gloucestershire village of Stonehouse. It was quite a distance from Vivianne in London, rural, and lacking in excitement. But I had Vivianne's visits to look forward to. The frequent commute was tough, yet we made the best of it, enjoying many weekends together in the idyllic British countryside.

What Stonehouse lacked in fun, it made up for with very relevant work experience. Stonehouse also gave me James Stuart, the best teacher, mentor, and supervisor that I could have wished for at that stage of my career. He understood the nervousness associated with my being relatively green in the field. I remember him assuring me that I would be fine, that I would achieve as much as anybody else and should make the most of my time there. With this assurance, I delved into work, investigating all the infectious diseases that occurred in the region, which included measles, tuberculosis, and meningitis. Stonehouse turned out to be a perfect place to work and learn as it offered limited distractions. I would work all week, looking forward to the weekend when Vivianne would visit, or I would make the trip to London.

I moved back to London when the EPIET programme was complete and was thrilled to be accepted into the public health specialisation programme that would enable me practise as a consultant in England. While the programme typically took five years to complete, my master's degree and the two-year experience with EPIET allowed me fast track my training and finish in three years. During those years, I worked in a variety of settings from local authority to regional health departments to national health organisations. I embarked on several missions for WHO, responding to outbreaks around the world. At the end of my training, I was employed as a consultant public health physician with the Health Protection Agency.

My work in England provided valuable experiences that would prove beneficial in the future. One such learning experience was the response to an *Escherichia coli* outbreak linked to an animal petting farm, which gained widespread media attention. I quickly learnt the importance of effective communication in managing public health crises. Disease outbreaks often become major public events, and utmost care had to be taken when briefing the media. In 2009, there was a H1N1 influenza pandemic, which was predicted to be catastrophic but thankfully did not cause as much harm as feared. I witnessed how a large-scale response to an epidemic was organised and managed. These events showed me that public health was a dynamic field, and being able to adapt and learn quickly was crucial to success.

As my career progressed, despite the excitement of my work in London, my heart was set on returning to Africa. In late 2010, I received an unexpected email at work, asking if any consultant would be willing to spend two years in South Africa to support the country's national public health agency. I was eager to hear Vivianne's thoughts on this, so I decided to seek her opinion immediately I got home.

"Would you like to move to South Africa?" I asked. Vivianne seemed somewhat perplexed by this question as South Africa had never been on our horizons. I had asked her the question even before settling down into our post work routines.

Without skipping a beat, she said, “That would be interesting.”

And with that, she breathed life and possibility into a completely spontaneous idea. We were open to it, albeit excited and nervous. In the meantime, I underwent the interview process that resulted in a job offer. A new frontier was opening.

It was an opportunity to gain new experiences and would bring us closer to our ultimate goal of returning home. We began online house-hunt, learning about the vibrant culture, the stunning landscapes, and the challenges of living in a country still grappling with its past. In February 2011, we moved to South Africa.

We slowly created a new life in Johannesburg. Vivianne enrolled in the MBA programme at the Gordon Institute of Business Science (GIBS), Pretoria; I was welcomed to join the senior management team at the National Institute of Communicable Diseases (NICD) in South Africa. My arrival caused quite a stir as my colleagues were surprised to find that the expatriate from the UK turned out to be a Nigerian. It surprised me to discover that even though apartheid had ended 20 years earlier, black people were still underrepresented in senior roles. Initially, I was the only black person at the senior management meetings, and I couldn’t help but wonder how some of my new colleagues perceived me, given the persisting strong notions about race in the country. Evidently, the rainbow in the Rainbow Nation wasn’t yet fully formed.

Initially, the situation was uncomfortable and made me question our decision to relocate. But as I settled into the NICD, my skin colour mattered less. After working with Professor Lucille Blumberg—the nicest infectious disease doctor on earth—I joined the Tuberculosis Department and together with my colleague, Nazir Ismail, we did some incredibly fulfilling work. Together with a really talented team, we implemented a study to measure the burden of drug-resistant tuberculosis cases in the country. This was a priority to shape new policy and treatment options emerging for TB. Nazir led the laboratory activities while I focused on the epidemiological aspects. My primary focus was on determining the population size needed for our study and to design the methods of implementation. Together with a really talented team, we conducted the most extensive survey on drug-resistant tuberculosis done anywhere in the world. We analysed the data, and published our work in the high-profile scientific journal, *The Lancet*. This attracted significant recognition for the institute and shaped the response to the tuberculosis epidemic in South Africa. Through the work done on this survey, I travelled all around the country, and got to understand in a lot more depth the opportunities and challenges that it had, but most importantly, I formed friendships and a deep connection to the country.

When my contract in South Africa ended, I didn't feel ready to return to the UK. Our family was comfortable in Johannesburg, with our sons thriving in their school routine and Vivianne's career on an upward trajectory after completing her MBA. I couldn't bear the idea of uprooting my family just yet, so I took an unpaid leave of absence from the Health Protection Agency in the UK and continued working for the NICD as a consultant. By supporting the NICD in setting up regional epidemiology services, I had the opportunity to do what I truly loved—mentoring and empowering young professionals to find their purpose and flourish.

During this time, I was invited by WHO to support the response to the Ebola outbreak in Liberia, and spent four months on the frontlines. The experience was both challenging and rewarding; it reminded me of the importance of public health and the impact it can have on people's lives.

5

MISSION TO CHINA

February 2020

I received a call from the Health Emergencies Programme of WHO asking if I would be available to join an exploratory mission to China. There was only one answer that I could possibly give and immediately agreed to join the mission.

Naturally, I wasn't one to shy away from responsibility and was always delighted by the prospect of acquiring new experiences. Being selected to join the exploratory mission was an honour; and, I would gain real-time insights into China's response to the emerging outbreak, which could aid the global response, including our work in Nigeria. After initial discussions, the mission was put on hold due to lengthy negotiations with the Chinese government.

WHO deployed its first high-level team of experts to China between February 16–24, led by Dr Bruce Aylward, a WHO Senior

Advisor. The findings from the joint mission would guide significant portions of the early global response and inform critical decisions on interventions, including the social measures that needed to be put in place. Unsurprisingly, I was the only African on the team. The joint mission team was a mini reunion as I had met some of my colleagues during previous work with WHO. I was reacquainted with Tim Eckmanns, a colleague I had worked with 20 years ago, during my very first job at the Robert Koch Institute. At the time, we were both working on antimicrobial resistance, which was Tim's focus. With the pandemic, we both had to drop our current professional interests and responsibilities to support the global response to the emergent virus. Tim and I hung out for most of the mission. There was also Maria Van Kerkhove, who I knew mostly for her work on the MERS coronavirus. We became friends while I was serving on the Strategic Advisory Group to WHO on Infectious Hazards (STAG-IH), where she briefed us regularly on her work on the MERS virus.

Bruce Aylward had spent several years leading the polio response efforts for WHO. During that time, the situation in Nigeria presented a major challenge for the global eradication efforts. I hadn't met Bruce previously, but I followed his work for years, given Nigeria's unfortunate status of being one of only three countries globally that had not yet eliminated the wild poliovirus at the time. He still had many memories of his work on polio elimination and we bonded over discussions on his work on polio and the challenges of working in Nigeria, especially around the disconnect between talent and delivery, in the public sector.

Figure 4: A meeting during WHO mission to China in February 2020.

Throughout the mission, Bruce was relentless yet polite in his approach, and I certainly learnt a lot from him. He constantly thought of new scenarios, assessing new hypotheses with persistent questions. We worked with 12 Chinese colleagues during the joint mission, scientists from different institutions across China. Given the objectives of the mission, there was palpable tension in the group. The face masks, which we had to wear all the time, dampened our communication by hindering the instinctive human connections that could only be established via facial expressions. Despite these, I was pleasantly surprised to discover that one of my Chinese colleagues spoke German, and we both had connections to Erlangen, a small city in Germany. Overall, I imagined that the Chinese colleagues might have been somewhat irritated by our many questions regarding the response; but they never lost their cool, and we never stopped asking.

As we travelled from Beijing to Chengdu, from Guangzhou to Wuhan, I marvelled at the scale of the cities. The infrastructure was simply mind-boggling, and it was hard to comprehend how a country that was until recently, relatively poor, could have done so much in so little time. During our work breaks, I made a conscious effort to learn more about this vast and complex country. I felt my knowledge of its history was inadequate and resolved to deepen my understanding. At the time, I still believed we would soon overcome the pandemic and things would return to normal.

I remember arriving in Wuhan on a train specially organised for us; there were no public transport links to Wuhan at the time of our mission. We spent the next day surveying what looked and felt like a ghost town, but on closer observation, realised there were people in every apartment and about 30,000 people in hospitals or under medical observation. The new virus had effectively shut down a city the size of Lagos. We visited hospitals and spoke to staff—some of whom had lost colleagues to the virus. They took us through the wards and offices in what sometimes seemed a carefully choreographed exercise, but at other times felt incredibly open and transparent. We spoke to several colleagues through translators and got mostly detailed answers. I was moved by the determination in their eyes and felt a newfound appreciation for the resilience of the human spirit.

In addition to the hospitals, we visited emergency operations centres and border posts, outpatient clinics as well as their public health departments. In these places, I noted the adherence to rules, the sheer volume of processes needed for the population size, and the ease with which most things were executed. We also visited residential blocks. I was intrigued by the self-organisation of the people and the structured leadership at every level. It was like nothing I had ever seen before.

I arrived in China with trepidation, unsure of what we would find. But what we saw was a country that had mobilised its resources to its fullest capacity. The streets were empty, people stayed indoors, and there was a pervasive calmness in the air. China had managed to implement these extreme public health measures so effectively, but also at great societal cost. The number of new cases declined, and we thought they may have subdued the virus in China. The intensive implementation of measures, later referred to as public health and social measures, seemed to have been successful. And it made sense. The likelihood of viral transmission is reduced when people are kept apart. This was what China essentially did, while using its systems to enforce it. The question on all our minds was whether other countries could do what China did, if this was what it took.

One thing was certain: if the measures implemented by the Chinese government were necessary to containing this pandemic, Nigeria was in big trouble. Our imminent departure from China stirred a queasy feeling in me. I was apprehensive about the consequences of this virus entering Nigeria. How would we cope with the immediate threat? But I had another thought on my mind. What would it take to foster the growth and development China had experienced in the last 30 years? I wasn't even thinking about infrastructure or bullet trains—none of that. What driving force made a country mobilise with such intensity around a shared goal? Was there more to it than met the eye?

Bruce Aylward briefed WHO leadership and the world of our findings before we left China. It was a complex situation to comprehend as we were all still learning about many aspects of this new virus and the impact it could have. Back home, I dutifully went into self-isolation per the country's requirement for travellers from countries with recorded ongoing transmission. I continued my work remotely, attending virtual meetings which had now become part of my daily routine, briefing my colleagues at NCDC and my principal, the Minister of Health. Things took an unexpected turn during my second week of quarantine. A sensational news headline from

Premium Times, one of Nigeria's digital news platforms, was in rapid circulation. It read:

CORONAVIRUS: HEAD OF NIGERIA'S DISEASE CONTROL CENTRE, NCDC, QUARANTINED—OFFICIAL.

Earlier that day, the Minister of Health had provided an update to the Senate regarding our preparedness plans. When asked why the DG of NCDC didn't accompany him, he disclosed that I was in self-isolation after returning from China without stating that I had followed all required protocols upon my arrival, including testing negative for the virus and adhering to the 14-day isolation. As expected, news outlets and journalists sensationalised the details, insinuating that I might have contracted the virus. This unwarranted attention and negativity were frustrating distractions from our important work. We had to issue a public press release clarifying the situation. I even had to tweet a photo of myself working in my home study as evidence that I was healthy and abiding by the rules. There was a lot of stigma around the disease at the time and while I wasn't personally worried, I was concerned about the impact it would have on our work.

The day after the news article was published, we received a letter from our son's school asking that he stay at home to protect other students because his father had travelled to China. We were deeply upset as this was in the middle of a school term. I was particularly worried about the stigmatisation he may experience at school. It was hard, but Vivianne took time to explain the situation to our children. I wrote to the school expressing our disappointment in how they handled the situation and focused on supporting our son with his work at home.

At this stage, the response leadership was in transition and a Presidential Task Force (PTF) was being proposed to manage the response. The virus was officially named Severe Acute Respiratory Syndrome Coronavirus-2 or SARS-CoV-2. I compiled a detailed report on my mission to China for our Minister of Health and was expecting an invitation to discuss in detail, but the invitation never came. I proactively offered to discuss the trip and provide my advice, but this too wasn't honoured. I found this strange and wondered if he was also worried about making contact with me. In my report to the Minister of Health, I concluded that we lacked the human and material resources needed to implement the measures to mount an effective response. If there were cases in Nigeria, we would find it very difficult to limit the transmission of the virus, given what I witnessed during the joint mission. However, I also noted that few countries in the world would be able to do what China did. I proposed an urgent and concerted mobilisation of resources to drive preparedness and response efforts. Nigeria has a strong national public health institute, a large network of trained epidemiologists, a partially rolled out electronic surveillance system, a national reference laboratory, and a committed public health workforce. It was time to get to work, and all we needed was the right support from our leaders, the public and other government institutions.

I never heard back.

One aspect of the response in China I found particularly intriguing was the clearly delegated authority from the leader to the communities around the country. This population-wide organisation and its associated structures were mobilised to deliver food items, medicines, and other daily items that people needed. An electronic surveillance system was in use to detect cases, enable rapid nationwide access to diagnosis, provide capacity for immediate case management and isolation, enable rigorous tracking, and isolate close contacts. Success depended on committed leadership and an exceptionally high compliance from the masses.

Achieving effective implementation of public health measures required an unusual and unprecedented speed of decision-making by leaders, operational thoroughness of public health systems, trust between leaders and engagement of society. Given the level of damage that was possible by uncontrolled, community-level SARS-CoV-2 transmission, such an approach was required to save lives and gain the weeks and months needed for vaccine development and testing of therapeutics.

By February 25, the virus which was first detected in Wuhan, Hubei Province, China in December 2019 had spread to 30 countries with a continued increase in local transmission reported in South Korea, Iran, and Italy. There were about 80,000 cases of COVID-19 reported worldwide. Of these, more than 77,000 confirmed cases were from China, with more than 2,500 deaths.

FLEDGLING STRUCTURES

2016–2020

Other than the newspaper story with the announcement, I had no other document confirming my appointment as the Chief Executive Officer of NCDC. With the help of my dear friend and colleague, Dr Sani Aliyu—who had also recently been appointed to lead another parastatal, the National Agency for the Control of AIDS (NACA)—I learnt that I had to pick up my letter of appointment from the Office of the Secretary to the Government of the Federation, which was within the confines of the Presidential Villa in Abuja. Since I had never been there, he offered me contacts and his driver. After several hours of formalities, the letter was extracted from a safe deposit box and handed to me. Armed with my official appointment, I felt more confident about approaching NCDC and beginning my work there.

My first approach was to consult with my predecessor at NCDC, Professor Abdulsalam Nasidi, a renowned virologist who had also been invited to lead the agency in its early years after retiring as a director from the Federal Ministry of Health. He was instrumental in pushing for the agency's establishment despite numerous obstacles. Professor Nasidi invited me to the IBB Golf Course in Abuja for our initial meeting, where he shared his valuable knowledge and experience with me. He gave me insight into his battles—some he had won—but many of which were still ongoing. It turned out that the very existence of NCDC was being questioned by many colleagues in its supervising ministry. The agency had a total approved annual capital budget of only N180 million—less than one million dollars at the time—and an overhead budget of N3 million for the year. This was nowhere near sufficient, yet I was determined to be creative about using our limited resources. I realised that I would need to fight for the survival of the organisation I had just been appointed to lead. However, I was certain that I did not have Professor Nasidi's capacity for battles and had to find another approach. Nonetheless, I was ready for the challenge and faced it with resolve; I had to try. For the NCDC team, and for the country.

During my first week at NCDC, I was gripped by strong feelings of nostalgia and anxiety. I felt an overwhelming sense of responsibility, knowing the future of public health in Nigeria was partly in my hands, but also partly beyond my control. I spent the week immersing myself in the system. I visited key stakeholders and NCDC's campuses—at that time there were two: one in Jabi, Abuja and the other in Yaba, Lagos. In Abuja, we had meetings at 8 a.m. to define our daily objectives, and the rest of the day was spent directly engaging staff. I needed to understand their roles, responsibilities, and challenges. While some were eager to share their ideas and enthusiasm, others seemed apprehensive and uncertain about their future in the agency. The staff member responsible for developing the epidemiological bulletin—a weekly summary of communicable diseases and disease outbreaks of public health importance—stated that the bulletin hadn't been produced for over two years. Revitalising NCDC would require not only addressing technical and logistical issues, but also rebuilding morale and trust.

The offices were poorly furnished and located in the middle of a residential area far from other Federal Government establishments. We had a handful of decrepit pickup trucks parked outside; the walls were dirty, and the roof was leaking. The entire place looked forlorn and depressing. It crossed my mind more than once that perhaps I had bitten off more than I could chew, and I wondered whether the best course of action would be to advise Mr President that the assignment was beyond the agency's level of development. The one thing that stopped me from giving up was the promise of transformation associated with my appointment into a new administration, and I was determined to make a difference.

One of the most important steps that I took at the very beginning was to invite colleagues who worked for the Tony Blair Institute (TBI) to work with us in developing a strategic plan for the agency. I had worked with TBI during the Ebola outbreak in Liberia and was impressed by their collaboration with the Liberian Ministry of Health in organising the structures and the response to the Ebola outbreak. TBI had also previously supported Kenya and other countries in improving their institutional capacity, so I figured we could trust them with supporting the setting of the strategic direction of NCDC. I also invited a colleague and friend, Dr Ebere Okereke, who worked for Public Health England, to join TBI on this project. Together with staff at NCDC, we developed the first strategic plan for the agency, articulating a strong vision for the organisation.

At the time of my appointment, there was no legal mandate or framework to guide our operations. This was particularly alarming given that we had narrowly escaped a devastating Ebola outbreak in 2014. Even though the Ebola outbreak was contained, there were visible limitations in our capacity to respond. Therefore, one of my first goals in the early days was to establish a legal mandate for NCDC, which was the first step towards ensuring adequate and stable funding. Although the Minister of Health at the time, Professor Isaac Adewole was fully supportive of this goal, not everyone in the Ministry of Health shared his enthusiasm.

It took almost two years for the NCDC Bill to make it through the Senate and House of Representatives. By this time, we had gotten to the public hearing stage—a standard step in the legislative process for bills—but it held immense importance for the future of public health in Nigeria. We received considerable support from several individuals and institutions within and outside the health sector. On the night before the public hearing, I received a leaked memo that had been apparently written by one of the other health parastatals, pushing back on some sections of the new NCDC Bill. I expected the contents of the leaked memo to be raised at the public hearing and was fully prepared to respond, but on the day of the public hearing, they weren't raised. The support for the new agency was overwhelmingly positive. I kept the memo.

After a long and arduous journey through layers of government bureaucracy, NCDC achieved a major victory on November 12, 2018, when the President of the Federal Republic of Nigeria gave his final assent, signing the Act to establish the Nigeria Centre for Disease Control and Prevention as a full-fledged parastatal. This was a significant milestone for the agency, as it finally had a solid legal foundation for its activities, which included improved access to vital resources such as specialised personnel and funding that could be independently managed. Thankfully, the new Act clarified the agency's responsibilities in key areas such as surveillance, outbreak response, developing a network of public health laboratories, and coordinating the training of field epidemiologists. With its new autonomy, NCDC was in a stronger position to provide technical support to states that needed it, as well as collaborate with other agencies to build up our capacity to detect and respond to public health threats.

Beyond our borders, the success of NCDC's emergence became a benchmark for other countries to establish national public health agencies of their own.

Deepening Structures

At the beginning of my tenure, the agency was severely understaffed, having less than 70 staff members, most of whom were deployed from the Ministry of Health. As an interim measure and to improve our functionality, I approached colleagues at the National Agency for the Control of AIDS (NACA) and the Nigerian Agency for Food and Drug Administration and Control (NAFDAC) to loan us staff members through a public service process called secondment. Luckily, the chief executives of these agencies were sympathetic and supportive, and I will always be grateful to them. With time, NCDC's reputation grew and colleagues from other agencies sought secondments as well. I had to manage these requests carefully to avoid being accused of poaching staff from sister agencies. Once this fledgling team was convened, it was time to empower them.

Agreements were drawn up with select partners like the US CDC, UK Health Protection Agency, University of Maryland (Baltimore), Georgetown University, and TBI to fully embed their staff in NCDC. This resulted in a highly collaborative environment where NCDC staff and partners worked as one seamless team towards a common goal. By the end of 2021, the agency had grown to 500 core staff, with another 100 working as consultants. In the early days, there were only two underactive technical departments: Surveillance and Public Health Laboratory Services. These two departments were woefully insufficient, thus, I created two new departments: Health Emergency Preparedness and Response, for dedicated coordination of the response to infectious disease outbreaks; and Prevention Programmes and Knowledge Management, focused on prevention and research, rather than simply responding to crises as they arose.

The most important currency of a national public health agency is the data it manages, which enables it to make informed decisions—hence, the need for surveillance and epidemiology teams responsible for monitoring the trends in new cases of diseases. When I arrived, this was mostly done through paper forms and at best, through the sharing of data on Excel Sheets. One of my early aspirations was the digitalisation of surveillance across Nigeria. We attempted this through the implementation of the Surveillance Outbreak Response Management and Analysis System (SORMAS), an open-source mobile web application software that enables the rapid notification of infectious disease. SORMAS was first introduced in Nigeria following the Ebola outbreak. It was expanded in subsequent years to support the management of other priority diseases following its adoption by NCDC as the platform for case-based disease surveillance for epidemic-prone diseases in Nigeria. The system offers mobile phone-based and web-based connectivity for all personnel involved in the process of notifying infectious diseases. It has been deployed in all states and Local Government Areas (LGAs) in Nigeria. As with the introduction of any 'new' tool, it was important that states were supported to fully adopt SORMAS as the backbone of infectious disease surveillance.

In 2016, NCDC also introduced an event-based surveillance system—supported by the University of Maryland in Baltimore, through a grant from the US CDC—to enhance the national surveillance system. The aim of this system was to rapidly collect and organise information about signals of events that are potential public health risks. Event-based surveillance in NCDC included actively trawling internet sources using a software called *Tatafo*—a Nigerian pidgin word for gossip—through incoming calls from the public via the Connect Centre, and by systematic searches of social media, blogs, health tracking websites, and news media. A toll-free number, as well as innovative approaches using SMS and WhatsApp messages, was introduced to improve public access to NCDC. By September 2016, the Weekly Epidemiological Record (WER) was reintroduced and shared publicly every week. The WER served as a tool for the rapid and accurate dissemination of epidemiological information on outbreaks of epidemic-prone diseases in Nigeria. Given frequent requests for data, we developed a National Disease Outbreak Dashboard in 2018. This dashboard features surveillance data from 2006 to date, updated annually.

To identify gaps in the country's health security capacity, we conducted our first Joint External Evaluation (JEE) of our health security capacities relating to the International Health Regulations in June 2017. The gaps revealed by the evaluation were addressed by the National Action Plan for Health Security (NAPHS), designed to cover the next five years. Developing the NAPHS facilitated Nigeria's access to extra resources, especially the World Bank's Regional Disease Surveillance Systems Enhancement project, providing a valuable opportunity for us to communicate our needs and priorities to our partners. I was fortunate to have the support of my colleague and dear friend, Chris Lee, during this process. As part of his work with *Resolve to Save Lives*, Chris frequently assisted NCDC, and his expertise proved invaluable in developing and implementing interventions led by our staff.

Figure 5: Signing off a World Bank facility to support the response at the state-level with the Governor of Ekiti State and the Chair of the Governor's Forum, Dr Kayode Fayemi. Photo credit: Ifeoluwa Ojo/IKP Studios

The preparedness and response department rapidly became the heartbeat of NCDC. The Bill & Melinda Gates Foundation's generous grant enabled NCDC to establish an Incident Coordination Centre (ICC) that now serves as a vibrant hub for public health information and analysis, as well as response coordination. To set this up, we converted a cafeteria near the entrance to our premises. I'm grateful to Valerie Nkamgang Bemo, Deputy Director, Global Development at the Bill & Melinda Gates Foundation. When partners lacked confidence in our institution, Valerie's support helped us establish the ICC and strengthen our public health emergency response capabilities. Without her guidance and dedication, our progress towards improving public health in Nigeria would have been much slower.

However, we knew that developing capacity in Abuja wasn't enough. In 2018, we began the establishment and equipping of State Public Health Emergency Operations Centres across Nigeria, to provide support and strengthen the capacity of these states. To ensure sustainability, we required the states to provide the building, preferably within the State Ministry of Health, which we then refurbished, equipped, and trained their staff. Commissioning these new centres allowed me to tour the country and engage with state public health departments.

The Department of Public Health Laboratory Services in Nigeria was ill-equipped and understaffed when I assumed office. Even though the National Reference Laboratory (NRL) was established in 2016, we were unable to test for multiple pathogens. In the following years, the NRL grew to become a regional reference centre for West and Central Africa, with the capacity to test for multiple epidemic-prone pathogens. It also has a bioengineering hub for the maintenance of laboratory equipment. The hub now has five bioengineers directly employed by NCDC and coordinates a network of over 100 public health laboratories across Nigeria. To promote expertise on specific diseases, we set up Technical Working Groups (TWG) to focus on specific diseases. These TWGs have become the lifeblood of NCDC's agile approach, facilitating preparedness alongside swift and effective interventions before, during, and after outbreaks. Each TWG comprised departmental representatives and relevant partners, which encouraged a collaborative and multidisciplinary approach to disease management.

Figure 6: A visit to the Bioengineering team at NCDC.
Photo credit: Ifeoluwa Ojo/IKP Studios

At the beginning of my tenure, Nigeria didn't have a strategic stockpile of essential commodities needed to respond to public health emergencies; we often waited for an outbreak to start before procuring necessary supplies. To bridge this gap, we began building and maintaining one in 2016. This stockpile has enabled NCDC to provide states with vital supplies such as personal protective equipment, laboratory supplies, and medicines during outbreaks. To further enhance the efficiency and effectiveness of the stockpiling system, we introduced a digital logistics management tool in 2019. This tool has significantly reduced the turnaround time between distributing, restocking, and monitoring of commodities in Nigeria. It has also enabled better resource planning and improved visibility of stock supply. Currently, the national strategic stockpile commodities are held in several NCDC warehouses in Abuja.

Figure 7: The interior of the new NCDC warehouse in Abuja.
Photo credit: Ifeoluwa Ojo/IKP Studios

In 2017, NCDC established a Department for Prevention, Programme and Knowledge Management. One of its responsibilities was managing the Nigeria Field Epidemiology and Laboratory Training Program (NFELTP), which had trained over 400 field epidemiologists as part of the Advanced Programme. This programme was initially established in October 2008 under the leadership of the Federal Ministry of Health, but funding and technical support was primarily provided by the US CDC through the African Field Epidemiology Network (AFENET), which managed and delivered the programme.

In 2020, NCDC undertook the momentous task of transitioning NFELTP from a donor-funded programme to one owned and primarily funded by the Federal Government of Nigeria, managed and coordinated by NCDC. This not only marked a major milestone in the history of NFELTP, but also presented an opportunity to evaluate the programme's achievements and adapt to changes in operational and governance contexts. This included the availability of technology, the maturation of its alumni, and other changes that may impact the programme. Despite encountering resistance from individuals who benefited from the management of a donor-funded programme, NCDC's commitment to this transition prevailed, ensuring that the programme continued to make significant strides towards building a resilient public health system in Nigeria.

In 2016, the threat of antimicrobial resistance (AMR) was looming large, yet Nigeria didn't have a strategic plan in place to tackle this growing public health crisis. I offered to coordinate Nigeria's response to this issue in one of my meetings with the Minister of Health, Professor Adewole. With his approval, NCDC established the National AMR Coordinating Body and convened a Technical Working Group (AMR-TWG) comprising stakeholders from various sectors. Through our coordinated efforts, we developed the National Action Plan for Antimicrobial Resistance (2017-2022), bringing together multiple stakeholders in the sector and paving the way for an enlightened approach to tackling antimicrobial resistance in Nigeria.

Structural Sustainability

A few weeks after I started at NCDC, my coursemate from medical school, Dr Tochi Okwor, requested a visit. She came with a group of colleagues who had been driving the development of the Infection Prevention Control (IPC) strategy in Nigeria, including Professor Sade Ogunsola, who would later be appointed as the Vice Chancellor of the University of Lagos—the first woman to hold this position. During their visit, they advised me to prioritise IPC, given the gaps and opportunities.

Hence, the National Infection Prevention and Control Strategy was established to address the consistent rise in the incidence of healthcare associated infections. This was followed by the launch of Turn Nigeria Orange in 2019—an IPC project aimed at improving the capacity of tertiary health facilities to minimise healthcare worker infections while managing infectious diseases. Later, NCDC created an online IPC course for health workers, on standard precautions, appropriate use of PPE, and other essential aspects of infection control.

Between 2016 and 2021, an internship programme and a library for staff was established, creating a well-defined process for research and knowledge management. NCDC internship includes two components: The Post-Baccalaureate Internship targeted at public health professionals with a bachelor's degree; and the Community Medicine Resident Internship for Community Medicine and Public Health resident doctors. These programmes have been highly revered by young people in Nigeria, who are keen on expanding their horizons and increasing their competitiveness in a tough job market.

When we first set out to establish the NCDC library, there were limited funds and enthusiasm. Our capital budget was miniscule, especially in the face of competing priorities like the purchase of reagents for laboratory and diesel to run our generators. However, a national public health agency needed a library, and I was committed to making it happen. I asked colleagues from previous organisations I had worked with to donate any relevant books or magazines that they didn't need; I was touched by their support and grateful for the contributions and the material that poured in. I still had to cover the significant cost of shipping these books to NCDC, but we found a way.

In 2016, PubMed—the database where all health-related publications are archived—showed that there were less than ten publications by authors affiliated with NCDC. In general, few Nigerian authors had led publications on prevalent infectious diseases. Instead, existing publications, were mostly authored by researchers from high-income countries, who then inevitably lead the discourse on infectious diseases in Nigeria. These publications hardly reflect the contributions of Nigerian authors to research processes, particularly those working in government institutions—a phenomenon known as parachute research: researchers drop in, conduct studies, and leave without appropriate acknowledgment, whereas researchers from high-income countries are perceived and recognised as the foremost experts on infectious diseases. They receive accolades, secure substantial grant funding, and are afforded speaking opportunities at prestigious conferences, reinforcing the notion of exclusive expertise. We established five key interventions in NCDC to address this:

1. We reintroduced the development of reports on all our surveillance activities, serving as the foundation for new manuscripts and providing valuable data for decision-making.
2. We prioritised, supported and incentivised the development of peer-reviewed papers with support from the Nigeria Field Epidemiology Training Programme, encouraging residents to document lessons and share them while enhancing their capacity.
3. We adopted a 'nothing for us without us' mantra in partnerships, ensuring collaborative manuscript development, with NCDC authors always being either the first or last authors and not just somewhere in the middle of the list. This was to promote ownership and inclusivity.
4. We established a research, training, and knowledge management unit at NCDC to support scientific writing and research collaborations.
5. Young staff members were empowered to proactively contribute to publications, with mentors providing guidance and ensuring their recognition as first authors.

By April 2022, NCDC had grown from having less than ten publications in 2016 to over 140. Of these, NCDC staff were first authors for 33 publications and last authors for 46. In addition to these peer-reviewed publications, NCDC staff led the development of annual reports, weekly situation reports during outbreaks, guidelines, and other technical documents. Our weekly epidemiological report lived up to its name, unfailingly published every week until I left NCDC in October 2021.

NCDC comprises of other non-technical departments that were leading the public health response to infectious disease outbreaks, Departments of Administration and Human Resources, Finance and Accounts, as well as Procurement, Legal, and Audit units. Like the technical departments in the beginning, they were understaffed and barely supported. I was shocked to discover, for example, that all our surveillance data were hosted by our partners. In fact, the brains behind our entire ICT Unit were two colleagues employed by a partner organisation. Staff members often used their personal email accounts for official communication, including the transmission of sensitive surveillance data. This wasn't unique to NCDC, as even officials in Nigeria's Presidency and Ministries communicated through their private emails. This lack of digital infrastructure hindered our progress, so I made it a priority to change things.

Within the first month of my tenure, we transitioned all NCDC staff to official NCDC email addresses. Initially, staff copied their private email accounts when sending me emails, but I made it clear that I would only respond to emails from official NCDC accounts. We also established an ICT Unit that grew rapidly in size and proficiency. Our first ICT staff member was Uche Iwuozor. This unit led a digital transformation that introduced a data security framework, transitioned data hosting from our partners to NCDC, and provided all staff with official computers and mobile phones to enhance data security. It was an arduous journey, but we eventually won over our staff. Their scepticism morphed into pride as NCDC became well recognised as a technologically advanced agency, meanwhile, we had only really done the very basics. But, NCDC is now fully equipped to host our surveillance data, and our ICT infrastructure can support our operations.

Figure 8: The first IT staff at NCDC, Uche Iwuozor.
Photo credit: Ifeoluwa Ojo/IKP Studios

As a public health agency, it was critical to have a platform for communicating to the public in a timely and efficient manner. When I joined NCDC, I was struck by the absence of a website and an active social media presence. Without a website, we were limited to transmitting information through hard copies or emails. Within the first three months of my tenure, we set up NCDC's website. It was a small launch event, but it was a huge milestone for us. NCDC's website became one of the very few websites managed by a government institution in Nigeria. It allowed us to connect with the public by sharing disease situation reports, weekly epidemiological reports, technical guidelines, vacancies, and other information. Over time, NCDC's website became a go-to source of information on public health in Nigeria, and I felt a deep sense of pride every time I attended global, regional, or local meetings, and information retrieved from NCDC's website was quoted. Our website never experienced any downtime throughout my years at NCDC, surviving many hacking attempts during the COVID pandemic and the number of visitors kept rising. But setting up the website was only the beginning. We also had to build an active social media presence to reach a wider audience.

We started using Twitter[3] and Facebook to disseminate information and engage with the public, and the response was tremendous. Through these platforms, we educated the public on disease prevention and control, dispelled myths and misinformation, and responded to queries. I'm proud of the transformation we achieved in our external communication, from a lack of website and social media presence to a reliable source of information for the public. Our commitment to transparency and accountability was reflected in the way we communicated, and I hope more government agencies will prioritise the use of websites and social media to connect with the public.

Besides our technical capacity, there was finance and procurement. I remember my first meeting with NCDC accountant very vividly. He was a hardworking and committed individual, which spurred my confidence in the financial report I was expecting. To my greatest surprise, he presented a stack of handwritten papers. Ledgers, pen, papers—I couldn't believe we were still at this stage. To make matters worse, the partners who were willing to support

3 On October 27, 2022, American businessman Elon Musk acquired the social media site Twitter and subsequently renamed it 'X'.

us insisted on passing their funds through a third party because our systems were just not good enough. Sadly, I had to agree with them.

Over the next few years, we overhauled our finance and accounts operations. We developed a Best Practice Manual and implemented a fully digital financial system using *QuickBooks*, which enabled us to manage our finances in real-time. The use of *QuickBooks* may not be phenomenal compared to other resource planning tools, but in the Nigerian public sector, it was no small feat. NCDC accounts team, led by Mr Abdullahi Buhari, exhibited an incredible flair for innovation while ensuring compliance with national regulations. I was overwhelmed with utmost pride when presenting our financial reports during donor meetings, and I couldn't be prouder of their progress. We have come a long way from those handwritten accounts.

Our Administration and Human Resources Department was also heavily reliant on files and paperwork—from accepting new staff, to managing and delegating authority, to applying for leave. This often resulted in long processing times, slowing down the overall effectiveness of the organisation. To improve this, we migrated to a digital HR platform, which streamlined our processes and boosted our productivity. With this platform, we could quickly process requests, manage employee leave, and ensure that information on staff needs was readily available.

Although we still had to adhere to the bureaucratic nature of the civil service rules—such as signing paper documents stored in hard copy folders—we could create a structure that ensured we remained agile and efficient in all our operations. Our Department of Administration, led by Mr Yakubu Abdullahi, was instrumental in driving these much-needed reforms. Despite the challenges, my secretary, Mrs Hwoja Jah, and the group of young people in the Office of the DG over the five years—Oyeronke Oyebanji, Tarik Mohammed, Ore Akomolafe, Nwaliweaku Anidi, Dabri Ohanu, Oluwatoni

Akinola, Ifeoluwa Ojo—stepped up and made a significant difference. Their hard work and dedication helped us modernise our operations and improve our efficiency. NCDC's transformation journey prior to the COVID-19 pandemic would later reflect the power of preparation in the battle against the unknown.

7

BLUEPRINT FOR FIGHTING PANDEMICS

2017–2021

All systems have a core that powers their operation, be it man-made or natural. When I joined NCDC, its abating core became more apparent to me during the 2017 meningitis outbreak in Northwest Nigeria, caused by the bacteria Neisseria meningitidis serogroup C.

The outbreak was spreading fast and highly fatal, especially among young children. As the Director General, I knew that urgent action was needed, but I was new on the job. I had inadequate resources to mount a robust response. We activated our emergency operations centre for the first time, and as with other disease outbreaks over the course of my career, I left Abuja and headed to Zamfara, the frontline. The lack of healthcare infrastructure caused scales of idealism to fall from my eyes. Centres providing care were comprised of essentially people, even children, being treated underneath trees whose branches held infusion bottles, the intravenous lines swaying carelessly in the wind while attached to the patients. When images of children receiving medication under the shade provided by trees were published on the front pages of most dailies, I expected outrage, condemnation, and a demand for accountability. But there was nothing. No impact. No pushback. There was no public outcry and no allocation of resources to address the situation.

While in Zamfara, I made several attempts to meet with the Governor at the time. He was never around, as his primary place of residence was said to be Abuja, which was over 500 kilometres away from his constituents. Another newspaper report featuring the Governor revealed that he attributed the outbreak to the wrath of God punishing the people of Nigeria for their sins. Everything unravelling at that point was a manifestation of what I had learnt over the course of my public health education and experience. Navigating outbreaks presents unknown, deep, and complex challenges. Cultural norms, societal attitudes, and uncanny leadership are dimensions to providing health care that are often unexplored in textbooks. Another dimension exposed by the outbreak was our overall lack of capacity to manage complicated clinical cases of infectious diseases in terms of testing needed for confirmation of meningitis symptoms and appropriate management. Almost every febrile illness was first treated as malaria, and an alternative cause of fever was only sought when this failed.

At the time, I desperately reached out to WHO and the US CDC; the latter offered to assist with testing. Due to security concerns however, the US CDC team couldn't travel to Zamfara and had hoped we could transport the samples to Abuja. But we didn't have a national laboratory in Abuja at the time. We explained to our US colleagues, with profound regret and embarrassment, that the country didn't have a functional national public health reference laboratory and had to turn down their offer. Eventually, WHO sent a team of scientists from the Medical Research Council in the Gambia, who could travel to Zamfara. They also agreed to remain in Abuja after the outbreak to support us in establishing molecular diagnostic capacity at our newly completed national laboratory.

Nigeria had received support to improve laboratory testing over the years, but testing was typically focused on specific diseases such as polio, yellow fever, HIV, and measles. Partners often provided reagents for testing diseases of interest to them and received data directly from these laboratories, with little involvement from the Nigerian government. In return, the laboratories focused only on the diseases of interest and associated programmes. In some cases, partners even paid the salaries of laboratory staff. This over dependence on partners to run our laboratories was deeply concerning to me, and I made it my mission to establish a national network. Each laboratory should be able to test for a spectrum of infectious diseases and not just diseases of interest. Many laboratories were eager to key into this vision, with two of the early laboratories in our network being the Irrua Specialist Teaching Hospital and the Alex Ekwueme Federal University Teaching Hospital, Abakaliki.

In 2016, the only laboratories the agency could claim as its own were a portacabin in Asokoro District Hospital, Abuja and a run-down Central Public Health Laboratory (CPHL) in Lagos. That was it. The portacabin laboratory had been established by the US CDC during the 2007 Avian influenza outbreak. It was then handed over to the Federal Ministry of Health, who passed it on to NCDC after its establishment. The CPHL in Lagos was in a state of utter disrepair. I was advised to visit the lab in person to understand the full extent of the problem. When I arrived in Lagos, I found a poorly lit, dingy laboratory with almost no functional equipment. Pieces of machinery that had clearly not been used for years littered the floor and tabletops. The medical compound in Yaba, Lagos, which housed the CPHL and several other government health facilities including a medical library, was in a derelict state. It was clear that time had forgotten this laboratory.

If one were to assemble a blueprint for fighting a pandemic, it would be impractical to exclude laboratory testing. NCDC couldn't be a credible national public health agency without a reference laboratory. It is simply impossible to contain, manage or control the spread of a disease whose pathogen cannot be categorised. Unfortunately, building and sustaining the quality of our public infrastructure has never been our forte in Nigeria. Almost every infrastructure managed by the public sector ends up in a dilapidated state. After the Ebola outbreak, strengthening our laboratory infrastructure should have become a matter of national urgency, but clearly, that wasn't the case. There was a glimmer of hope when my predecessor, Prof. Abdulsalam Nasidi, secured a building in Gaduwa, Abuja to serve as a reference laboratory.

We visited the building in August 2016. It was completely empty and filled with dust. The dislodged ceiling boards gave it the semblance of a ghost town. We gave ourselves a year to revamp this dispirited building to a functional National Reference Laboratory (NRL). The goal was to ensure that it could support surveillance activities as well as our response to outbreaks. The meningitis outbreak meant that our developmental plans had to be fast tracked. I shared the vision of a rehabilitated National Reference Laboratory with Dr Adebayo Adedeji, the Director of the Laboratory at the time. Dr Adedeji was fully onboard in theory, but he had reservations. He just didn't believe it was possible within the timelines that I had set. Our team, with support from the US CDC, the MRC Gambia team led by Professor Antonio Martin and his able assistant Catherine Okoi, and every individual we could find to support our vision, commenced the rehabilitation.

To show our dedication, we shut down the existing portacabin in Asokoro. Within a week, we cleaned up the laboratory building in Gaduwa, arranged for power and water supply, and set up the basic infrastructure required. We commenced an intense period of training. I spent my weekends at the laboratory, often bringing lunch for everyone. Finally, on May 31, 10 months after I started leading NCDC, the first diagnostic tests were carried out at NCDC NRL. It was a proud moment for all of us. We had a functional national reference laboratory! This event marked the beginning of a new era for public health services in Nigeria.

Figure 9: Catherine Okoi and colleagues looking at the results of the first tests carried out in NRL.

With NCDC NRL set up, we assumed our role as the country's public health coordinating laboratory. Our responsibilities included coordinating the network of existing laboratories that carried out diagnostics for various epidemic-prone diseases. Nigeria had a long history of battling Lassa fever, which was discovered in the country over 50 years ago. Each year, the capacity to respond was weakened by the inadequate laboratory infrastructure. But with a functional and credible national public health laboratory in operation, we could now support states to improve their public health laboratory capacity, especially those with a high burden of Lassa fever.

We supported Ebonyi State to operationalise the laboratory at the Alex Ekwueme Federal University Teaching Hospital, Abakaliki (AEFUTHA), leveraging the human resources at the Irrua Specialist Teaching Hospital (ISTH) to train their counterparts in AEFUTHA. Soon after, the Federal Medical Centre in Owo, Ondo State was up and running too. Our laboratory network was growing, and partners were very supportive, and together, they supported the expansion of the laboratory network in Nigeria. We also supported these three hospitals to establish and strengthen their infectious disease case management capacity. In 2018, we carried out a nationwide training on Lassa fever management because at the time, most states in Nigeria sent their Lassa cases to ISTH for treatment. We needed to decentralise this capacity.

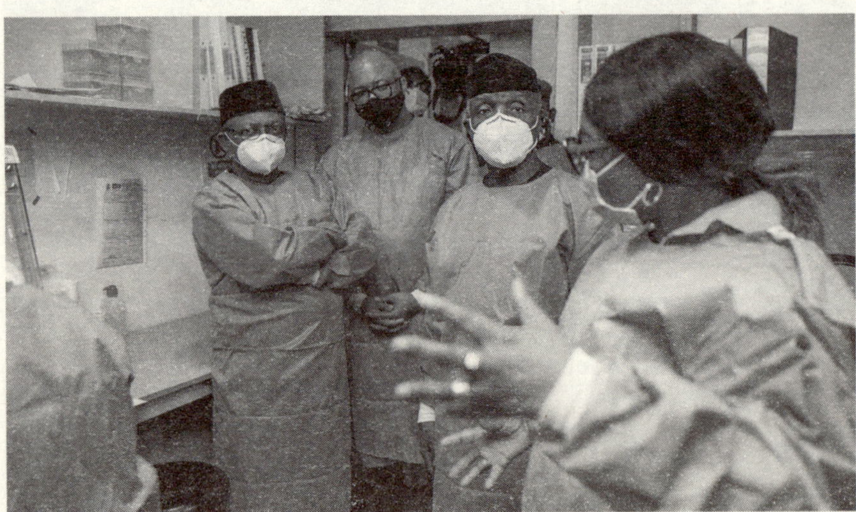

Figure 10: The Former Vice President of the Federal Republic of Nigeria, His Excellency, Professor Yemi Osinbajo during a visit to the National Reference Library. Photo credit: Tolani Alli

Establishing laboratories meant we had to figure out how samples would get to the lab for testing. We set up a sample collection system to transport samples collected from state capitals to the public health laboratories in our emerging network. It may sound easy in principle, but setting up an efficient, safe, and reliable sample transportation system required a logistics system wherein each sample was safely collected and stored appropriately and tracked from the time it left the health facility to when it reached the laboratory. This had never been done in the public sector. We found a small courier company, trained them and worked with them to deliver the service we needed. Another piece of the puzzle was falling into place.

After operationalising the NRL, we turned our attention to the staff and the laboratory space. A conducive working environment was required. We started retraining our staff, many of whom had never received any prior training. In the process, we realised that we needed a biomedical engineering team to ensure proper maintenance and repair of our equipment, but skilled professionals in this field were scarce. All over the country, you would find hospital wards and laboratories burdened with malfunctioning equipment that have been abandoned due to minor faults.

Several interviews later, we found a fresh graduate with minimal experience, Innocent Okoli. Despite his limited practical experience working in laboratories, Innocent had a lot of enthusiasm and was eager to learn, so we hired him as an intern. Some of my colleagues thought I was crazy, but I saw potential in Innocent and encouraged him to take charge of setting up the biomedical engineering team at NCDC. Following his employment, we learnt that no other laboratory within our network had a bioengineer. Once again, I leveraged on our partner network for support and was able to convince the Japan International Cooperation Agency (JICA) to train Innocent in Japan for three months. During his time there, he gained hands-on experience in the repair and maintenance of various medical devices.

Innocent returned to Nigeria brimming with newfound knowledge and ideas. He played a key role in setting up NCDC biomedical engineering hub, which eventually grew to a team of five members. It was a remarkable achievement—a testament to Innocent's hard work and dedication. His story serves as a reminder to me, that when we provide the opportunity for our young people to grow, the possibilities are endless.

A pandemic response blueprint, even one with a functioning laboratory system, is incomplete without surveillance. In public health, surveillance data is collected over years, counting people with diseases and other related data points. Historically, we collected this data through a mix of paper and Excel-based notifications. A Disease Surveillance and Notification Officer (DSNO) in a local government area receives reports of a suspected case of a disease and begins filling a paper-based form with the details of the case. The form is then stored until the next routine inspection or visit by the State Epidemiologist. In some cases, the information was recorded on an Excel sheet, and sent through the levels of government to NCDC. This manual process of data collection and entry was not only slow but also prone to errors, making it difficult to analyse the data and respond effectively to outbreaks. We had to urgently modernise our surveillance systems.

In the wake of the West Africa Ebola outbreak in 2014, a colleague, Gerard Krause with whom I had worked over 20 years ago, along with a group of colleagues at the Helmholtz Centre for Infection Research (HZI) in Germany, worked with members of our Field Epidemiology Training Programme to develop a digital surveillance system called *Surveillance, Outbreak Response Management and Analysis System* or SORMAS. It enabled web-based connectivity on handheld devices, allowing for the immediate notification and validation of infectious diseases.

We pushed for the immediate implementation of SORMAS by training state personnel and providing them with Android devices, SIM cards, and data. We prioritised states with outbreaks, where having a digitalised disease notification system would enable us to respond rapidly. SORMAS was a game-changer, and we were finally confident in reporting our infectious disease data. It completely changed our interaction with colleagues at state levels as we could see data being reported in real-time. In 2018, we published a paper on how time delays in the response to the 2017 meningitis outbreak contributed to preventable deaths. But with SORMAS, we could coordinate a more efficient response. This built confidence in our organisation. Bit by bit, our systems were beginning to work against all odds, and it was an incredibly empowering feeling for all our staff.

Once the map of an outbreak has been created with surveillance data, coordination is required to mount an efficient and successful response. In 2016, Nigeria lacked a National Public Health Emergency Operations Centre (EOC) which led to fragmented responses during disease outbreaks. To address this, the NCDC Incident Coordination Centre (ICC) was established in September 2017, using funds from the Gates Foundation grant that we had received. The ICC served as the focal point for daily activities involving the detection of new outbreaks, and functioned as an EOC when an outbreak response was activated. By the end of 2020, we had responded to over 20 disease outbreaks.

The establishment of the ICC was another pathbreaker for NCDC's operations. It became the hub of our activities, with daily tasks ranging from intelligence gathering, to monitoring, to outbreak preparedness and response activities. The centre's agility and flexibility were vital in managing public health incidents, and it became a critical asset to NCDC. It was the first place we took our visitors because it was easy to demonstrate the process of detecting and managing disease outbreaks.

We decided to introduce this approach at the state level, but needed to ensure that every state had a stake in what we were offering. Before establishing an EOC in a state, we required them to provide a dedicated building for the State PHEOC, ideally located within the Ministry of Health, and to integrate it with the Department of Public Health for effective coordination. NCDC would provide assistance in terms of furniture, equipment, and staff training and development. Our goal was to ensure that each state had a functional PHEOC capable of quickly detecting, responding to, and controlling outbreaks of infectious diseases and other public health emergencies. This model has been successful in improving outbreak response and preparedness activities in several Nigerian states.

Figure 11: A meeting at NCDC's Incident Coordination Centre.
Photo credit: Ifeoluwa Ojo/IKP Studios

With states in the country establishing their PHEOCs, complemented by SORMAS and the establishment of public health laboratories, NCDC developed the *Strengthening States for Health Security Strategy* in 2019. It emphasised the need for each state to establish an infectious disease treatment centre and provide the Office of the State Epidemiologist with the necessary resources to carry out their duties. By the end of 2021, we had achieved a significant milestone in supporting all the State Epidemiologists in the country with vehicles to facilitate their work. While it is typically the responsibility of state governments to provide resources for their epidemiologists, we recognised that limited resources and competing priorities could make this challenging for some states. With the additional resources made available through the pandemic response efforts, we were able to step in and provide support, ensuring that State Epidemiologists in *all* states can mobilise to sites and carry out their important work, including disease surveillance, outbreak investigation, and response coordination.

In the early days of the coronavirus pandemic, a significant gap in the country's healthcare system was revealed. Many states hadn't prioritised their responsibilities in strengthening health security, and this became evident when state governors began calling me directly to request NCDC's support in setting up laboratories or infectious disease treatment centres. At the onset of the pandemic, there were only seven public laboratories in the country available for molecular testing. Despite all our efforts prior to the outbreak, NCDC was heavily criticised for the lack of testing capacity in states. To address this critical need, I quickly put together a team at NCDC to support states in establishing their laboratories. Our team, including our group of young biomedical engineers, spent most of 2020 on the road, travelling across the country to support the set-up of new molecular laboratories. Setting up a new laboratory involved not only equipment installation, but also training scientists and other personnel, and supporting them with data management. This was a complicated process, and we couldn't afford to make mistakes.

A public announcement was made for every lab we opened, and this generated a momentum that continued to grow as the response to the pandemic progressed. We received feedback from states, lauding the positive impact of the laboratories in their communities. However, setting up these laboratories wasn't without risks. For example, early in the pandemic, we had to advise that the laboratory in Kano be shut down when staff were getting infected from what appeared to be non-adherence to biosafety requirements. This was one of the consequences of rapidly establishing molecular laboratories, while responding to a pandemic.

In hindsight, the work we did with these laboratories was crucial in enabling an effective response to the COVID-19 pandemic. It also highlighted the need for states to take ownership of their responsibilities in strengthening health security.

8

THE INEVITABLE

February–April 2020

Nigeria, as we learnt, was no stranger to outbreaks. Every single month, there was a cluster of infectious disease cases emerging in different parts of the country. But the COVID-19 pandemic was different. It was new, and it was spreading at an alarming rate.

Serendipity might seem like a romantic or idealistic concept, certainly not a term one might associate with a life and death scenario like the impending arrival of a rampaging virus, but in hindsight, it felt like everything that had led up to this point, all the twists and turns over the years, the challenges faced and overcome, the systems we had built from nothing and sustained, made it possible for us to face what was to come.

Our incident management systems and structures at the NCDC Emergency Operations Centre had been functional since 2016.

With the news from Wuhan, we quickly activated our emergency operations centre and appointed an incident manager to take charge. We hoped to do all we could to keep this virus out of Nigeria. As our understanding improved, we had to acknowledge that keeping the virus out of Nigeria would be impossible, so we rechannelled our focus towards preparedness. Information and guidelines were rapidly changing; preparing for the virus was like building a ship and sailing it at the same time. Our immediate goal was to develop and implement prevention and preparedness plans, while keeping close tabs on the situation unfolding in China and the rest of the world. It wasn't just about protecting our own people. We had a responsibility to the global community to prevent the virus from spreading.

After our COVID-19 Preparedness Group developed a detailed plan, the problem of funds arose. We submitted our plans and budget to the Minister of Health, who was supposed to pass it on to the President. Days turned into weeks, yet nothing. I was worried that my Minister wasn't giving this threat the attention it needed. I had a responsibility to protect the Nigerian people, and I had to find a way to surmount the bureaucracy of the government. So, I took a bold step and went straight to the Presidency. It wasn't an easy move. I expected it would ruffle feathers, and I was right. It caused some tension that I was bypassing the usual channels, but sometimes, even in our beloved country Nigeria, one must put the needs of the people above bureaucratic red tape. Protocols, formalities, biases, personal grievances—all that does not matter when our collective survival is threatened. It turned out that the Presidency had been waiting for us and was actually dismayed that it had taken us so long to ask. I kept the reasons to myself.

At that point, NCDC didn't have an outbreak response fund, except a limited revolving fund provided by *Resolve to Save Lives*—a non-governmental organisation founded by former US CDC Director, Tom Frieden—but it wasn't designed for major events like the COVID-19 pandemic. I had been trying for years to set up a similar fund within NCDC, but it never gained traction with our leadership. Instead, we were forced to rely on begging for funds from our partners every time there was a crisis. I was incredibly frustrated and disappointed that our leaders had taken our resilience for granted, assuming that we would always be able to solicit funds in times of crisis. NCDC shouldn't have been put in a position where its usefulness depends on its ability to raise funds from external partners in response to a crisis. It was like expecting the fire service to seek water vendors in search of water to be gifted when there was a fire.

Every other day in February, a new country reported its first case, increasing the global incidence. Part of our initial focus was strengthening screening measures at airports and developing guidance to enlighten passengers on the risks involved. While this was primarily the responsibility of Port Health Services—a unit in the Department of Public Health in the Federal Ministry of Health—they had even fewer resources than we did at NCDC and were unable to do this by themselves. NCDC funded the printing of leaflets and supported the staff of Port Health Services in deploying and collecting data from passengers. Our concern extended to case detection and transmission prevention. All prospects had to be considered.

We leveraged information gathered from WHO and other sources to develop public health messages aired on local media stations, despite our limited knowledge of the emerging virus. I mandated every member of the NCDC team to remain informed, read up on the virus, follow up on news updates, and inform me of significant updates. In anticipation of a surge in demand, we sought out colleagues to support our work. I invited Dr Assad Hassan and Dr Kelly Eliman to join us on short-term contracts—excellent colleagues who could bring 100% focus to our initial response, as we needed that kind of commitment. Dr Assad was the State Epidemiologist for Kebbi State, while Dr Elimian was an academic from the University of Benin Teaching Hospital. Both had worked with us in the past and hit the ground running, immediately.

As the virus continued to spread, anxiety and scrutiny of returning travellers from China intensified. Even people of Chinese descent who hadn't left Nigeria for years were stigmatised, and we had to deal with calls from concerned citizens who demanded immediate investigation of Chinese nationals for all sorts of reasons. The NCDC Connect Centre would regularly receive calls from people informing us that they had just spotted an individual from China in their neighbourhood, requesting someone from NCDC to investigate. Sometimes people took the situation into their own hands and confronted their neighbours. It was a tough situation, but we did our best to educate and reassure people and discourage stigmatisation.

Looking back, one of the earliest gaps in the response in Nigeria and other countries was that surveillance was disproportionately focused on China. Given what I saw during my visit and the extraordinary measures that China was taking to limit the spread, I was somewhat less concerned about China at this stage. Nevertheless, we were quick to provide travel guidelines for passengers coming from China to Nigeria, maintaining surveillance and recommending isolation for 14 days. This measure was introduced as early as February 3. For other travellers, we simply advised them to adhere to recommended safety measures and report to designated hospitals if they felt ill. At that point, I began to really worry about the increasing number of cases in Europe, but was initially reassured because the cases reported in the UK—the biggest travel destination for Nigerians in Europe—were still apparently low. Reported cases in Europe were initially concentrated in the Lombardy region, an area in northern Italy. It was slowly becoming obvious that this new epidemic was spreading at an alarming rate, and we couldn't afford to focus only on China.

Meanwhile, news reports from other countries showing images of people on ventilators and in hospital wards instilled fear in Nigerians. The average Nigerian could sense that the country's poorly equipped and inefficient health system would struggle to cope with a potential influx of critically ill patients. At NCDC, however, we tried to remain calm while pushing on the areas that we had influence over. We focused our attention on the next stage of preparedness: testing capacity.

At this time, NCDC had a reasonable stockpile of personal protective equipment, given that the COVID-19 outbreak was occurring at a period we would normally be experiencing an upsurge in Lassa fever cases. But the supply chain for laboratory reagents was inefficient. We reached out to our traditional partners at WHO and the Africa CDC. I knew that global demand for their support would be very intense, so I also reached out to colleagues at the Robert Koch Institute (RKI), who agreed to immediately send reagents to test the first few cases. We split the first reagents between NCDC National Reference Laboratory (NRL) in Abuja and the University of Lagos laboratory, which was managed by Professor Omilabu, a long-standing collaborator of NCDC who played a key role in the detection of Nigeria's first Ebola case in 2014. Finally, we could officially announce that we had the capacity to test and confirm cases here in Nigeria. This announcement significantly changed the perception of NCDC's preparedness.

Throughout February 2020, there were multiple false alarms with reports of individuals showing symptoms of respiratory illness after returning from countries with ongoing transmission of COVID-19 cases. Initially, the only country in this category was China, but gradually, more countries were added to the list. NCDC chose a cut-off of people returning from countries with over a 1,000 cases as those that would receive extra checks at the airport on arrival into Nigeria. The call centre's capacity was rapidly expanded, and colleagues in

Port Health Services joined us to call passengers returning from these countries to check if they had any COVID-19 symptoms since their return.

One evening, I received a call about an Ethiopian Airlines flight enroute to Kano with a passenger who was coughing and had a high fever. The State Epidemiologist was notified, and colleagues went to the airport in personal protective gear to wait for the plane. The ill passenger wasn't allowed to disembark, was stabilised on the aircraft, and flown back to the country of departure. Similar cases continued to pop up over the next few weeks, and each time I received a call from Professor Omilabu in Lagos, I thought: *this is it.* But it wasn't. The anxiety associated with the anticipation of the inevitable was almost crippling.

In the meantime, NCDC continued to develop preparedness plans and build capacity locally; part of which meant my involvement in several discussions about the growing outbreak and response strategies. Together with 20 scientists from around the world, I was privileged to be a member of WHO's Emergencies programme's Scientific and Technical Advisory Group on Infectious Hazards. Through discussions in this group and with colleagues at WHO, I developed my analysis of the situation in Nigeria. I was also part of an informal group convened by Dr John Nkengasong, Director of Africa CDC, to support the coordination of prevention and response efforts across the continent. He made a tactical move, asking select countries to lead preparedness in specific areas; Senegal and South Africa led the development of laboratory capacity, while Nigeria led infection prevention and control. Courses were organised to train laboratory scientists and technicians on the diagnosis of the new virus, and in what had to be the shortest time ever from ideation to implementation, a team was sent to Senegal to participate in the training for the laboratory diagnosis of SARS-CoV-2.

Prior to the outbreak, NCDC had initiated the development of the first modern infectious disease ward in the country at the University of Abuja Teaching Hospital, Gwagwalada. We had spent years convincing stakeholders that this type of facility was needed, at least in the Federal Capital Territory. We had Lassa fever cases in mind when building the hospital facility and wanted to hedge against a future Ebola outbreak. It had male, female and children's wards, and provision for its own operating theatre, laboratory, pharmacy, morgue, and all other facilities required to efficiently manage severe infectious disease cases, away from other patients.

The building was only halfway complete when the pandemic began, leaving us ill-prepared to manage a potential first case in Abuja. To address this, we worked with the Chief Medical Director of the hospital to convert a recently developed casualty ward into an interim COVID-19 facility. We managed to source beds and equipment, and even transported a generator from the NCDC office to the hospital. We considered it more important to have a ward ready in Abuja than a generator in our office. The brutal race against time was in full swing.

Figure 12: The new Infectious Disease Treatment Centre at the University of Abuja Teaching Hospital, Gwagwalada. Photo credit: Tijesu Ojumu

In early April, we were invited to the National Assembly on one of several missions concerning the outbreak. There, the Chair of the Presidential Task Force, who was also the Secretary to the Government of the Federation, made a headline-grabbing statement:

> *"I can tell you for sure, I never knew that our entire healthcare infrastructure was in the state in which it is until I was appointed to do this work."*

Understandably, it led to an uproar when reported. How could a senior government official claim to be ignorant of the state of our healthcare infrastructure? It was plain as day to citizens and the government that the healthcare sector had never received the attention it deserved and required. With the imminent arrival of an unknown virus, citizens began to place health and healthcare at the centre of the political agenda, scrutinising the country's preparedness and response capacity. A salient point was made: sustained investment in public health infrastructure and emergency preparedness was no longer negotiable, albeit, too late for this pandemic. Nonetheless, NCDC worked creatively within its sphere of influence, strengthening screening measures, developing public health messages, and identifying potential cases to prevent further transmission. We established testing capacity in several labs, including NCDC National Reference Laboratory; the virology laboratory of the University of Lagos; the Nigerian Institute of Medical Research; and the Africa Centre for Genomics of Infectious Diseases. We were in the process of bringing on board three other laboratories, the Irrua Specialist Teaching Hospital, Federal Medical Centre, Owo, and Alex Ekwueme Federal Teaching Hospital, Abakaliki, to start testing suspected COVID-19 cases. Along with these measures, we developed guidelines for the notification of cases, case management, laboratory testing, and communication in anticipation of the inevitable first confirmed case. But there was another underlying factor that had potential to mar our preparedness plans. Lassa fever.

Lassa fever cases are recorded year-round in Nigeria, with the peak period usually between December and April. Many NCDC colleagues with significant outbreak response experience were already deployed to states for the Lassa fever response; our top three infectious disease treatment centres in Edo, Ebonyi, and Ondo were full of Lassa fever cases. State Epidemiologists were also occupied with investigating and responding to Lassa cases. In the same week that Nigeria's first COVID-19 case was eventually reported, we had 109 confirmed Lassa fever cases with eight deaths from 19 states.

The final feature of our delayed preparedness plans was a simulation exercise to practise our response to a potential case in Nigeria. Simulation exercises were a crucial part of our work at NCDC. In 2018, we collaborated with the West African Health Organisation to organise the largest-ever yellow fever simulation exercise in West Africa, which involved colleagues from the Republic of Benin. These exercises provide a chance to assess our capabilities, identify gaps, and generate additional evidence for increased attention and funding. They also offer the opportunity of collaboration with other government institutions in a near-real-life setting.

We planned for a simulation exercise to take place between February 27–28, supported by WHO Nigeria Country Office—*Resolve to Save Lives,* colleagues from the African Field Epidemiology Network (AFENET); the US CDC; World Bank, and Public Health England. We also typically invited other agencies such as the Nigeria Civil Aviation Authority (NCAA) and the Federal Airport Authority of Nigeria (FAAN) to join our simulation exercises.

It was at this point, in the middle of a simulation exercise, that the call came. The inevitable had happened; the novel coronavirus had made its way across our borders.

SYNCHRONICITY

"No person is safe until all—everyone, everywhere—are safe, and no country is safe until all countries are safe. Only by working together can we ensure that no one is left behind."

Amina J. Mohammed

THE FIRST WAVE

February–March 2020

Day 1/Case 1

Late in the evening of February 27, my phone rang.

Professor Omilabu was calling from his laboratory in Lagos. He had just received the test results from a patient who had recently returned from Italy.

"DG, I think this is it."

With a sinking feeling in my gut, I promised to call him back shortly for further details. I was exhausted from the intense preparedness activities, the constant reporting required to be sent to our leadership, engaging with international colleagues and organisations, pushing for increased budget to support our preparedness, and the fear of our limited preparedness in states. But once the call came in, adrenaline took over. We activated our emergency response systems and within hours, they were mobilised to begin contact tracing, testing, and isolation. This was the beginning of a long and challenging journey for Nigeria's public health system, but it was a journey we were ready to embark on. We knew that the stakes were high and were determined to do everything in our power to protect our citizens from this deadly virus.

The confirmation call came in later that night, and my mind was consumed with the crucial calls I had to make. I reached out to other medical colleagues involved in managing the patient, gathering all the necessary details about the case. Next, I called Dr Tomi Coker, the Commissioner for Health, Ogun State, where the Italian passenger had been diagnosed. The patient had initially reported to a private company's clinic feeling unwell, and the astute Dr Amarachukwu Allison recognised the potential danger, quickly collecting the right sample. When the diagnosis came back positive for the SARS-CoV-2 virus, Dr Allison made the decision to transfer the patient to Lagos for treatment, given the limited facilities in Abeokuta. The next call I made was to the Commissioner for Health, Lagos State, Professor Akin Abayomi, to ensure that all necessary steps were being taken in the treatment of the patient.

With the support of these two colleagues and our comprehensive preparedness plans, I was ready to make the most critical call of all—to the Minister of Health. After updating the Minister on the details of the case, it was time to alert the international community. This wasn't just a significant development for Nigeria but also for the entire West African sub-region; it was the first case in the sub-region and only the second African country after Egypt to report a confirmed case. I made calls to WHO African Regional Office (AFRO); Africa CDC and the West African Health Organisation (WAHO). In those moments, the importance of timely and accurate communication couldn't be overstated. The world was watching, and every decision made could have a significant impact on the trajectory of the pandemic. The leaders of all the regional health organisations were appreciative of hearing directly from me and gave credit to Nigeria.

After communicating with health leaders, it was time to disclose the news to the public. I advised the Minister of Health to draft a press release that same night and release it before morning to enable us stay ahead of the situation from the outset. Keeping anything lowkey in Nigeria is almost impossible, and the spread of information can be fast and unpredictable. It was crucial that Nigerians received the correct information from the appropriate authorities at the right time. Our goal was to ensure that Nigerians had as much information as possible, while being advised on necessary actions to take to avoid panic. Fortunately, the Minister of Health accepted this advice. I personally drafted the press release with the help of our directors at NCDC. Vivianne supported me through the night, reviewing the drafts to set the right tone, language, and message, informing Nigerians of the situation while allaying their fears and providing reassurance.

To ensure effective communication, we set up a COVID-19 crisis communications team. Once news of the first case came in, I alerted them on our WhatsApp group that it would be a long night, and I needed their full support. They stayed up, carrying out various tasks, including designing the accompanying visuals to communicate the information through our various channels in a timely, clear, and effective manner.

While gearing up to announce the first COVID-19 case, the big question surfaced. Who would make the announcement? My friend and colleague, the Lagos State Commissioner for Health, believed that Lagos State should announce the case, given that it was confirmed in a laboratory in Lagos State, and the patient had been transferred to a treatment facility there. However, I firmly believed that the announcement of the first case in Nigeria had to be made at the national level, to demonstrate strong central coordination and leadership by the Minister of Health, and to emphasise the seriousness of the situation. Moreover, the patient was identified in an Ogun State facility before being transferred to Lagos State. After several hours of discussion, we agreed that the Minister of Health should make the announcement. This was one of many instances that exposed the vagueness of powers and responsibilities on national and state level, within the context of a federal republic managing a national emergency.

The Ministry of Health didn't have a social media team in place, so the small crisis communication team at NCDC had to lend a hand. Getting the login details for the Ministry of Health's Twitter account was tricky, as the person who had it was asleep. With help from the Minister's Technical Assistant, the account login details were found, and all was set.

Tijesu Ojumu—an excellent young colleague in our NCDC communications team, who was working from home—alerted me to the power outage in his house. His laptop's power was running out, and he needed to continue working. Tijesu started as a corps member at NCDC and eventually became responsible for designing the infographics used to announce the first case, and several hundred others over the course of the pandemic. He was just one example of young colleagues who started their career at NCDC and grew to take on much more responsibility than was usual for someone with only a couple of years in service. An official car and driver was deployed to pick him up from his apartment and bring him to NCDC office. We then powered the office generator to ensure we could continue working through the night.

At exactly 11:36 p.m. on February 27, the Minister of Health posted a tweet that we had drafted for him, announcing Nigeria's first confirmed case of COVID-19. The NCDC communication team was also on standby and less than five minutes later, we shared the tweet using NCDC's account. Thus, the famous graphic of NCDC

COVID-19 updates was born. By midnight, the full press release signed by the Minister of Health was shared on NCDC website and all media houses on our roster. I spent the rest of the night speaking with my communications team, the EOC, and the Commissioners for Health in Lagos and Ogun State. We went to bed at 5:00 a.m., totally drained. After a short nap, I woke up at 6:05 a.m. to keep pushing, fuelled by anxiety and adrenaline.

The events of that night really made it clear that at critical moments, especially in a health emergency, fast and effective communication is critical. If we had waited until the morning to share details of the first confirmed case, there would have been a risk of the information leaking out and the details of the first confirmed case being miscommunicated.

The reaction to the announcement was immediate and intense. Within minutes, the news of the first confirmed case of COVID-19 in Nigeria had spread like wildfire across social media platforms. People were anxious and frightened, and many were unsure of what to do. The NCDC hotline was flooded with calls from concerned citizens seeking guidance and information. The response from the public wasn't surprising, given the widespread fear and panic that had gripped the world since the first reports of the virus emerged from China. The initial response to NCDC's tweet was mixed. While some expressed concern about the first confirmed case, others doubted its existence. Some blamed the government for not shutting down the airspace earlier, and when it was closed soon afterwards, the government was heavily criticised for the timing of the closure. At this point, any decision made attracted opposing viewpoints.

Over the next few days, we focused on providing accurate and up-to-date information to the public through various channels, including social media, traditional media, and direct engagement with communities. With people already expressing doubts about the existence of the virus, we had to keep our ears close to the ground and create channels of communication that provided accurate responses to what was being said. One tweet read:

> [The NCDC only announced the case] as a plan to gulp down the 300 million+ [naira] mapped out by the government to combat coronavirus.

This prompted me to tweet from my personal account later that night, calling for Nigerians to focus on #FactsNotFear. Prominent Nigerians also spoke up, including Dr Oby Ezekwesili, who publicly declared her trust in the NCDC team. Her solidarity was a great and timely boost for us. We held press briefings, radio and TV interviews, and town hall meetings to educate people on the virus, how it spreads, and what they can do to protect themselves and their families. One morning in early March, I woke up to news that airlines had started evacuating foreign nationals out of the country—an alarming sign of the times. While the official reasons weren't directly related to an increase in the risk of transmission in Nigeria, there was anxiety about access to appropriate healthcare services in Nigeria, especially critical care. The condition of Nigeria's tertiary healthcare facilities didn't assure the governments of these nationals that they would receive adequate treatment if the worst were to happen. Additionally, foreigners developing symptoms would put more pressure on the already strained healthcare system.

The preparations for our pandemic response were now in a frenzied state, as we struggled to keep up with rapidly evolving recommendations from WHO. We tried to reassure Nigerians that everything was under control, even though the authorities were struggling on multiple fronts. The first confirmed case had travelled on an aeroplane with other passengers, arrived in Lagos and then travelled to Ogun State where he resided. He had also interacted with colleagues in his firm before presenting at the clinic; his contacts demanded testing. The test kits we had weren't enough to meet the expected demand.

The morning after the first case was confirmed, we immediately escalated the NCDC EOC from Level 1 to Level 3—the highest alert level. Given that we had managed many outbreaks in the past, we had developed a seamless understanding of incident management systems. Faced with the bureaucratic nature of public service, and despite the excellent work Dr Olaolu Aderinola had done as Incident Manager in the preparedness phase, I decided to make a more senior, director-level colleague the Incident Manager, while Dr Aderinola became Deputy. One of many reasons for this was the need for the Incident Manager to regularly brief the Minister of Health. The Director of Preparedness and Response, Dr John Oladejo, was then appointed to lead the EOC.

About the same time, I sent an email to all NCDC staff asking that all of the agency's resources be fully redirected to the COVID-19 response and requested other agencies to support our efforts. I was flooded with emails and phone calls, especially from media houses requesting comments on our activities. This prompted the development of a list of frequently asked questions (FAQ). Within three days of the first confirmed case, we published this FAQ in major Nigerian dailies and shared it on all our platforms. These were updated throughout the response. On my recommendation, the Minister of Health agreed to host a press briefing the next day, February 28.

The press briefing provided an opportunity to address initial questions and demonstrate the willingness of government officials to make themselves available at a time when there were still many unknowns. Despite the general lack of trust in the government, Nigerians had to put their doubts aside and support NCDC. The response to the emerging threat could only succeed with collective effort from all members of society.

I asked the Incident Manager to urgently deploy a team to Ogun and Lagos States to support their initial response; thus, the first Rapid Response Team was constituted. They departed Abuja on the first available flight to Lagos, with drivers awaiting their arrival. All airline tickets were privately funded to be reimbursed after memos had been signed and approved. When the team, led by Dr Oladipo Ogunbode, arrived in Lagos, half of them proceeded to Ogun State to support with contact tracing, while the other half remained in Lagos. The WHO Country Office also deployed colleagues led by Professor Adebola Olayinka to support NCDC Team.

During those first few days, my focus was on harmonisation. I made countless phone calls to create networks for managing the index case and subsequent ones. Dr John Nkengasong sent support staff with test kits to aid our immediate response. After speaking with colleagues in WHO, US CDC, and other national public health institutes around the world, I came to a stark realisation. Although many offered to help, everyone was immersed in a similar response in their own countries and couldn't do much. Things were likely to get worse over the next few weeks, but more than that, we would be largely on our own.

Despite protocols on how to respond to a first case being in place, the advice on what to do afterwards was changing on a daily basis. The initial recommendation from WHO was to test only close contacts—defined as people within two seats in every direction from the confirmed case and the cabin crew in an aircraft. Through our contacts at the airport, the NCDC call centre obtained the passenger manifest of everyone who arrived with the index case and started calling passengers. Most passengers were eager to get tested, as this was the only way to be certain they weren't infected. Due to the shortage of test reagents, I had to make a tough, unpopular decision to test only those who needed it, not everyone who wanted a test as a means of reassurance. People called government officials to mount pressure on me, but I stood my ground. NCDC had become a trusted source of reliable information, so we felt certain that our recommendations would hold sway with the public.

We focused on advisories for foreign travellers to Nigeria, as well as people travelling abroad from Nigeria to limit spread. Passengers travelling to and from Nigeria were screened for fever using the thermal scanners maintained since the Ebola outbreak. Travellers seeking entry into Nigeria were placed in three categories based on the transmission level in the countries they were travelling from. Our recommendation at the time was that travellers from countries with sustained transmission—there were only five of them at the time—were advised to stay at home for 14 days even if they didn't have symptoms. We advised that they contact the NCDC call centre if they developed any symptoms, which would warrant testing to confirm infection. Travellers from other countries were only expected to adopt non-pharmaceutical measures such as handwashing and physical distancing.

I was in constant contact with my colleagues across the states—particularly State Commissioners for Health and Chief Medical Directors (CMD) of our tertiary public hospitals—joining the WhatsApp group of CMDs and the Commissioners for Health. NCDC team developed documents for these two groups, including case management guidelines, case definition for identification, and our answers to FAQs. I provided my direct phone number and that of my assistant. Being personally available to support the needs of the State Commissioners was key to the success of our response, a fact still acknowledged by all parties till this day.

The next few weeks would be the start of a marathon with no clear ending. We had to recognise that the identification of a case in Nigeria wasn't a sign of failure; more than 40 countries globally had reported cases at the time. It certainly reflected the adage that 'infectious diseases do not respect borders.' This was a novel infectious disease that was bound to spread, driven by multiple factors outside anyone's control. From the first week after the first confirmed case, we started publishing a daily situation report, informing Nigerians of the number of cases, where they were identified and the status of our response.

On March 21, we decided to change from reporting new cases in real time to daily reports. State Epidemiologists across the country would carefully collate their confirmed cases and send these figures to NCDC where they were crosschecked, verified, and signed off by the Incident Manager. Only then would the data be communicated to the public. This measure ensured NCDC's credibility as the trusted source for all information related to the COVID-19 response and mitigated rumours from other media outlets. I communicated to all NCDC staff that we would be transitioning to a seven-day work week. Normally, I would need the permission of the Head of Service to do this, but I decided to act now and apologise later.

Through it all, NCDC remained committed to a rational, evidence-based approach and prioritised the needs of the people. While the journey ahead was uncertain, we were steadfast in our mission, knowing that our efforts would impact the lives of millions.

10

THE INTERFACE OF POLITICS AND POLICY

March 2020

Day 8/Case 43

As the initial response to the emerging pandemic gathered steam, the Chief of Staff (CoS) to the President of the Federal Republic of Nigeria, Malam Abba Kyari—a man known for his wit and proactiveness—delved into the scene.

On Saturday, March 7, he convened a group of senior government officials, including ministers who would have a role to play in the response and a few heads of agencies. The CoS, who had just returned from a trip to Germany where he had gone to negotiate a new power sector deal for the country, seemed calm and collected, despite the gravity of the situation. There were no fancy refreshments, just a few bottles of water and groundnut, a testament to how quickly the meeting had been set up. We talked for hours, discussing the implications of the emerging pandemic on the economy, security, and governance of the country. He listened carefully to everyone's opinions and ideas, and soon enough, initial action plans emerged. We agreed to reconvene the next Saturday with the Lagos State Commissioner for Health, Professor Abayomi, in attendance. The meeting ended late at night, and we dispersed.

Dr Sani Aliyu, the former Director General of the National Agency for the Control of AIDS, as well as my supportive friend and colleague, was on a private visit during the onset of COVID-19. We met and brainstormed on how to get better alignment and coordinate the multisectoral response to the pandemic. The CoS invited both of us for a discussion that birthed the idea of a Presidential Task Force (PTF) to coordinate the cross-government response. Chief, as we called the CoS, immediately recognised that this couldn't be left for the health sector alone and took responsibility for organising the instruments of government to respond. We were tasked with drafting the terms of reference of the PTF, while he proposed the composition and its leadership. Subsequently, he took the proposal to Mr President, and the Presidential Task Force on COVID 19 was born, with a lifespan of three months to deliver the response.

Saturday came, and we reconvened for another meeting as agreed.

This time, the meeting started with lunch, and Chief looked a bit sniffly—seemingly unwell, despite managing the meeting with his usual rigour. After the meeting, he asked me to arrange a COVID-19 test for him. We were still in the process of setting up sample collection centres across the country, but I immediately arranged for a member of the NCDC sample collection team to collect a sample from him privately. The test was run on Sunday at the NCDC National Reference Laboratory, and the initial results came out positive. I was shocked and asked for it to be done again. We gave the CoS an excuse about the laboratory equipment not functioning optimally and requested that he give us another sample, which he did on Monday morning. We also advised that he stayed at home while we carried out the second test. By that evening, the result was out. It was undoubtedly positive.

I arranged for a meeting with Dr Aliyu at my office at NCDC. He knew that something was wrong and came over immediately. We agreed to meet the CoS at his home that same evening after I explained the situation. We started making calls to see Chief around 9 p.m., and soon after, we made our way to his home. On the way to Chief's house, in addition to the difficult news that we were about to convey, I was thinking about the bottle of groundnuts that was passed around during our first meeting. I tried to remember every single person in the room. My heartbeat quickened. I pushed the thoughts to the back of my mind. One thing was clear. The next few days were going to be tough, but first, I had to get through tonight.

As I stepped into the sparsely furnished government bungalow that served as home to the CoS, I couldn't help but notice the worn out red carpets and old-fashioned air conditioners. A tray of tea and biscuits sat on the centre table, but my mind was focused on the task at hand. We sat across the CoS to break the news. Together with Dr Aliyu, we gave him an overview of the situation; and explained the implications, asked about his health, and that of his wife. He still was sniffling but didn't seem to be experiencing any severe symptoms at the time. We discussed where he may have been infected and concluded that it must have been during his trip to Germany. He assured us that he would let his staff know and of course, advise Mr President. At the time, there had been only 42 confirmed cases in Nigeria. The CoS was case number 43.

A team with my most trusted staff was immediately dispatched to test Mr President and his family, as well as Chief's immediate contacts. Before the team left, the seriousness of their mission and the importance of discretion was clarified. I placed one of my most experienced virologists, Celestina Obiekea, in charge. I had great confidence in her clinical and communication skills. It was only a matter of time before the CoS' positive test became public knowledge, and I needed to be prepared for the inevitable questions about the President's health. We obtained a list of high-risk contacts and tested them, hoping that the information wouldn't leak before it was officially announced.

Once the President and his family tested negative, the CoS himself announced that he had tested positive for COVID, sending the media into a frenzy. The situation continued to spiral and became increasingly difficult to manage. As things evolved, I skipped a crucial step: informing the Minister of Health of the CoS' positive test. I struggled between privacy considerations of my patient in this case, including his explicit insistence that I keep his result private and my responsibilities of informing my Minister. I was caught between a rock and a hard place, but ultimately decided to respect the privacy of my patient, given that there were no public health consequences of doing so in this case. When the Minister heard the news of the CoS' positive test, he called me immediately, very upset, speaking in a way that I had never experienced before. He was furious that I hadn't kept him in the loop as the situation unfolded. I tried to explain the context, the chaos and sensitivity, with which the test was done, but it was a lost cause. I understood that there was a hierarchy in government, but I also had a duty of confidentiality to my patient, which in this case was the CoS. My innate instincts as a doctor had simply won over the adherence to a chain of command. In the end, I realised that an important relationship had been strained, and I don't think I was ever forgiven for it. But I had to live with that and move on; there were more pressing issues at hand.

The Presidency in Abuja was a busy place, and the CoS was constantly meeting with important people. There was an entire group of very worried VVIPs who wanted to be tested, but they didn't want to go to any of the recently designated testing centres at the National Hospital and the University of Abuja Teaching Hospital. Instead, they wanted their samples taken discreetly on their own terms. My phone was ringing non-stop. We quickly set up two teams to visit high-profile people in Abuja, collecting samples and sending them to the laboratory. Our preparation was paying off, as we managed the stream of requests efficiently and provided results. Many of the VVIPs insisted that their names be excluded from the details on the sample collection bottles. I even offered to test our Minister of Health and his family, hoping to ease the tension between us. This was done with precision, and I hoped it relieved his anger in some way.

Throughout this period, I stayed in touch with the CoS. He was following the evolution of the outbreak in Europe closely, sending me WhatsApp messages with his thoughts and ideas on how we should respond. We would debate the utility of his suggestions against the backdrop of the country, but he was never overbearing, always ending by acknowledging that we were the 'experts.' After a while, his messages became less frequent, and I began to worry. Eventually, I heard that he had been transferred to a private hospital in Lagos as a precautionary measure. I was concerned, but I kept my fingers crossed. Somehow, through the adversity we had faced, a close relationship had developed between us.

By mid-March, the pressure began to take a toll on me. I was constantly receiving messages and phone calls, and it was impossible to respond to everything. This made me do something I never thought I would ever do. For the first time in my public service career, I switched off my phone. It was the only way to think and focus. But I still needed to stay in touch with my team at NCDC and my family, so I got a second phone with more controlled access.

Given my close contact with the CoS when he tested positive, I had to take drastic measures to protect my family. It was a difficult decision, but I moved into our guest room and isolated myself from

Vivianne and our boys. Living in isolation was tough, but it was even tougher knowing that my family was just on the other side of the door. It was a constant battle of wanting to be close to them and keep them safe while also knowing that I needed to be responsible and not risk infecting them. My sons were fully aware of what was happening. Even as children, we were very open with them. I felt guilty for not being able to give them the attention they deserved. Before isolation, I would often leave for work before they woke up and come home after they had gone to bed. Even in isolation, I worked late into the night and was constantly on the phone with various people, trying to gather as much information as I could. After my test results came back negative on two separate occasions, I finally moved back into our bedroom, craving the comfort and assurance of Vivianne. I could tell she was anxious as well, but we both knew we had to do our best to shield our boys as much as we could. It was one of the most difficult periods of our lives.

Before the CoS fell ill, he had established the PTF as discussed, and it ended up being a turning point for NCDC during the pandemic. It provided a direct line of responsibility to the highest level of government. When I took over the leadership of NCDC, I faced many challenges with our parent Ministry. It had taken nearly ten years for NCDC to go from an idea to an actual agency, and during that time, our key responsibilities were being handled by the Ministry of Health. Even after NCDC became a fully-fledged parastatal, certain parts of the Ministry never fully accepted this reality and wanted to exert undue operational control over our work. Given my resistance to this situation, I didn't have too many friends in the Ministry. But I knew that our mission was more important than friendships, so I remained resolute. In most countries, the national public health agency is the technical agency responsible for the surveillance of infectious diseases and leading public health response measures. The Ministry of Health is responsible for developing policies and providing strategic oversight. Prior to NCDC, I had worked my way up national public health agencies in three countries, so I knew the drill.

As the pandemic raged on, the Ministry of Health insisted on taking over certain operational responsibilities, including case management. The justification for this was that the Department of Hospital Services (DHS) which oversaw the tertiary hospitals was within the Ministry's purview. After several meetings, we reached a compromise. The DHS would handle case management, but would operate within the EOC coordinated by NCDC. The DHS introduced a new reporting system separate from the existing surveillance system for infectious diseases that NCDC was championing. There was no technical capacity to fully implement this, and it caused chaos. Hospitals across the country were asked to move their reporting to a new system in the middle of a pandemic. It was incredibly difficult for people who were already overworked and exhausted; hence, the data flow was disrupted and never recovered, and opportunity to integrate hospital data lost.

President Muhammadu Buhari formally inaugurated the COVID-19 Presidential Task Force (PTF) on March 17, 2020. I was appointed to the PTF, along with the DG of the Department of State Services (DSS) and several ministers. The DSS DG and I were the only parastatal level appointees. At first, I didn't know what to expect from this new responsibility even though I was grateful for the political attention the response was receiving.

Figure 13: Members of the Presidential Task Force on COVID-19 in a meeting with the President.

I previously had little direct engagement with the SGF (Secretary to the Government of the Federation), Mr Boss Mustapha, before the pandemic. With him chairing the PTF, I became a regular part of his office. He remained calm and led an evidence-based response, even in the face of significant provocations and radical ideas. For example, there was a particularly intense phase in the pandemic response when 'magical cure' stories began circulating. People were grasping at straws—even the government of Madagascar was promoting an apparent cure for COVID-19, which was rumoured to be endorsed by the President. Some suggested we stockpile chloroquine, despite the lack of evidence to support its effectiveness against COVID-19. The SGF was under immense pressure to follow suit, but he remained firm, took advice and made decisions based on science and evidence, not politics or pressure. His ability to unite various ministers under such immense pressure was exemplary. His leadership capabilities were truly impressive, and I will always respect him for that; although sometimes, I wished he had been more assertive with decision making.

On March 23, we woke up to the sad news of the first COVID-19 related death in Nigeria. The patient had been a former manager in one of Nigeria's key parastatals and had an underlying health condition which was exacerbated by the virus. This news amplified the severity of the pandemic, especially as it came on the same day the last commercial flights into Nigeria were allowed to land.

Less than a week later, my colleagues and I were glued to the television at the National EOC, listening to President Muhammadu Buhari address the nation. My heart was racing with anticipation. At some point in the address, Mr President mentioned my name, recognising my role as part of WHO delegation to China. I was grateful for the opportunity to share my knowledge and expertise and the confidence it brought to Nigerians. I felt a deep sense of pride knowing that I was part of a team that was working tirelessly to protect our nation and its people.

The President delivered his message with the confidence that Nigerians desperately needed; he was calm and measured, urging the country to adhere to the advice of NCDC. He announced the cessation of all movements in Lagos, Federal Capital Territory, and Ogun State for an initial period of two weeks, exempting essential services. He also announced that all flights in the country were suspended except with special permissions, and all schools and universities were closed. The Ministry of Health was requested to deploy staff of Port Health Services to the road boundaries in and out of the affected States. A moratorium of three months was given on all Federal Government lending, and Mr President assured that there would be other measures to ease the pain of citizens. Finally, he called on Nigerians to take personal responsibility and promised that the government would do whatever it took to confront the emergent epidemic, and to adhere to 'NCDC Guidelines', a phrase that will be repeated across many sectors for the next two years.

We were in uncharted territory. The airports were shut, there were no commercial flights, and our elite had nowhere to run to. It was a very unusual situation for the Nigerian elite who were well-known for flying out of the country to access healthcare. For the first time in our history, Nigerians of all social classes would all have to manage whatever the country had to offer. We had deployed a rapid survey to assess the ICU beds in Nigeria, and the results were shocking. There were less than 300 functional critical care beds in Nigeria, with most of them having sparse access to oxygen. This was a disaster waiting to happen, and we had to act fast. My team and I were going to do whatever it took to confront this emergent epidemic. As days turned into weeks, and weeks into months, I saw first-hand, the incredible resilience and strength of the Nigerian people.

On the morning of April 18, I boarded an aircraft afforded to us by the Nigerian Air Force, ready to embark on a hectic national tour. We had finally started receiving some of the resources we needed to respond to the COVID-19 pandemic, but there was still so much to be done, especially in the States. My plan was to assess the preparedness in the states and ensure they had everything needed to respond effectively. We put together an ambitious plan to visit two states per day for a one-week schedule that would end up in Lagos.

Figure 14: On supervisory visits to the States supported by the Nigerian Air Force. Photo credit: Ifeoluwa Ojo/IKP Studios

As I settled into my seat, ready for take-off, my phone rang. The Chief of Staff to the President had passed away the night before, and his body was on its way back to Abuja for burial.

I immediately called our infection prevention and control team, instructing them to be on standby to support the funeral activities. I also updated the Minister of Health on the measures we were taking. A cloud of worry plagued my thoughts as we flew into Imo State. The Chief of Staff's funeral inevitably meant there would be a crowd—a nightmare for the already overwhelmed healthcare system. We had to be proactive to prevent the situation from worsening. The death and transportation of Chief's body was managed by the security agencies, and NCDC wasn't informed of the arrival of his remains in Abuja, particularly the timing. We were however aware that in keeping with the Islamic faith, he would be buried as soon as possible.

When we landed, the Governor of Imo State, Hope Uzodinma, sent a team to pick us from the airport. Throughout the day, I kept one eye on the affairs before me and another on what was going on in Abuja, trying to stay abreast on the funeral arrangements. We commenced our meeting with the Governor by observing a minute of silence for the late CoS. As the day aged, calls kept coming in. Over 4,500 calls were received on NCDC toll-free line that day. Despite the challenges, I was proud of our ability to respond to the crisis, mobilise resources, and keep the people informed.

The funeral of the CoS, attended by most members of the Presidential Task Force, was a sombre occasion. The crowd of mourners was huge and not well-managed, raising concerns about the possible spread of the virus. Later that day, I received disturbing WhatsApp videos of some undertakers discarding their personal protective overalls within the funeral grounds, and the general public believed these were NCDC staff. I alerted the funeral team at the FCT public health department, and they sprang into action. They collected and properly discarded the personal protective equipment. This was just one of several social media incidents that often distracted us from the immediate response, but we remained focused on our goal.

The death of the CoS was a tough blow, but we had to keep going. After Owerri, I headed to Anambra State where I met with Governor Willie Obiano. We discussed the difficult decision to close Onitsha Main Market, which was causing him and the traders severe economic pain. Onitsha Market is the nerve centre of commerce in the southeast of Nigeria and one of the largest commercial markets in West Africa. It was hard to imagine a scenario where it would be closed for much longer. I realised that the economic implications of the pandemic were just as significant as the health implications, and we had to acknowledge this reality in our response efforts.

In Rivers State, we were received by a delegation sent by Governor Nyesom Wike himself. It was a relief to know that despite his adversarial position with the Federal Government, he was willing to work with us in this fight. We were hosted at the State House, but uncharacteristically, Governor Wike said very little. At the small welcome reception in the Government House, I made my comments, then his Commissioner for Health spoke. Governor Wike then called for the national anthem to close the event and thanked me for my visit. My colleagues assured me that this was a good thing; at least he had received us and listened to what we had to say. From the Government House, we moved to the State Ministry of Health for detailed discussions.

The reception in Delta State was much warmer. Governor Ifeanyi Okowa's background as a medical doctor and as previous Chair of the Senate Committee for Health had clearly given him an advantage in preparing his state for the pandemic. In Katsina State, it was encouraging to see that so many people were willing to take the COVID-19 test, but we encountered challenges with the facilities for care and treatment. In Kano State, for instance, there seemed to be a large undetected outbreak going on, and even some of our colleagues working in the EOC got infected. The EOC had to shut down temporarily, and the coordination structure fell apart for a while. Even the Commissioner for Health ended up in isolation. Many states seemed to have taken their lead from the Federal Government to set up task forces to manage the response, often parallel to state public health teams. We met with Governor Abdullahi Umar Ganduje who expressed his commitment to the response. Our visits to the states were very brief, yet important, given the need to ensure that all states were fully aware of the situation and that the response was being led by the highest level of government at the state level.

In the early weeks of the response, news circulated that many high-level government officials had tested positive for the virus, possibly contracted during trips abroad. While some were forthcoming and shared their results publicly, others decided not to. I strongly encouraged those who had tested positive to be transparent about their infection, as this would encourage others to get tested. We also stressed the importance of isolating in government facilities to prevent the spread of the virus. By the end of 2020, at least seven governors, several ministers, and members of the Senate and House of Representatives had tested positive for COVID-19. Of course, we knew all of them, but the majority of officials who had tested positive chose not to disclose their test status publicly, which put others at risk. Senior colleagues even demanded that I reveal the identities of those who had tested positive. I always maintained that patient confidentiality was paramount, and that I would only disclose information with their consent or in exceptional circumstances where public safety was at risk. One senior colleague, following my refusal to disclose this information, severely berated me and warned me to be careful.

Another interesting development was the sudden emergence of the so-called 'Air Doctor virus blocker tag' in the Nigerian market, which claimed to offer virus-blocking capabilities. At one point, it seemed everyone was wearing this badge on their clothing, including several government officials. When asked to comment on the matter, I told the media that there was no evidence to support the tag's effectiveness in preventing the spread of the virus nor any indication of biological plausibility. Our sister agency, the drug regulatory agency in Nigeria, NAFDAC, also released a similar statement. Unfortunately, some governors and ministers continued to appear in public wearing the tags. This was an illustration of desperation and the challenge we faced, trying to communicate accurate information about the pandemic to the public. The number of cases continued to rise daily, and we worried about the resilience of the structures we had put in place to manage the crisis. By day 34, there were 131 confirmed cases.

In late April 2020, the House of Representatives suddenly announced a new infectious disease bill sponsored by the Speaker himself. While the bill was intended to provide an updated basis for the government's pandemic response efforts, it gave me, the Director General of NCDC, enormous powers. Additionally, the wording of the bill closely resembled a similar law in an Asian country, leading to accusations of plagiarism against the National Assembly. I had never seen a draft of the bill, nor was I consulted on it. As the leader of NCDC, I was uncomfortable with the situation, but I knew that respect for the National Assembly was paramount for the evolving democracy in Nigeria. Sahara Reporters, one of Nigeria's more outspoken online news websites, in an article headlined "Nigeria's Proposed Infectious Disease Act: Plagiarised And Dangerous", included a subsection in the article titled:

DIRECTOR-GENERAL OR UNELECTED DICTATOR?

I had to clear my name and that of NCDC. An invitation to appear before the House provided the perfect opportunity to do this. NCDC had done credible work with the response, at least in the eyes of many Nigerians, so Members of the House weren't generally hostile towards us. When I was called up by the Speaker to address the bill, I found myself in a tricky situation. I couldn't contradict him in full view of the cameras, but I also couldn't agree with the bill's contents. I managed to avoid answering the question directly, insisting that now wasn't the time to analyse legal frameworks, while acknowledging the Speaker's positive intentions. I also suggested that any changes in legislation be made through a more consultative process, involving many additional stakeholders that would include the public, private sector, and civil society. He pressed further, but I thanked him for his inspiring leadership of the House of Representatives through a period of crisis. He let me leave the stand, and I was relieved. I understood his sentiment towards finding ways to strengthen Nigeria's response to infectious disease outbreaks; however, I didn't feel that was the right time. Besides, changes in legislation had to consider different views through consultation.

Throughout the pandemic, I attended many meetings with the Senate and the House of Representatives, answering questions on all aspects of the response. I was privileged to brief the President on our progress, alongside the SGF and Chair of PTF; my friend and the National Coordinator, Dr Sani Aliyu; and the Minister of Health. It was always an honour being in his presence, and I was struck by his apparent rapt attention, even though he didn't say much. He listened cautiously as we presented the latest scientific information and recommendations, and it was obvious he had been following our work closely, likely watching us on the Nigerian Television

Authority (NTA) channel. One time, he even asked us to convey his appreciation to the Minister of Information, Alhaji Lai Mohammed, for the excellent coverage of the PTF's activities on the NTA channel.

Otherwise, he spoke very little about the content of our reports. While the President was often criticised for being too quiet and delegating too much responsibility, I believe his approach to our work in this instance was fitting. He seemed to trust our discretion and gave us the space we needed to do our jobs effectively. He delegated sufficient authority to the Secretary to the Government of the Federation, who took the task very seriously. This was especially important when we saw other world leaders getting overly involved in the response and promoting unproven treatment methods. In those cases, their involvement often hamstrung the efforts of their scientific advisers, and we were able to avoid the politicisation of the response.

Looking back at my time with the PTF, I feel a deep sense of gratitude for the President's trust and support. We were left to focus on what was most important: protecting the health and well-being of the Nigerian people during a difficult and uncertain time.

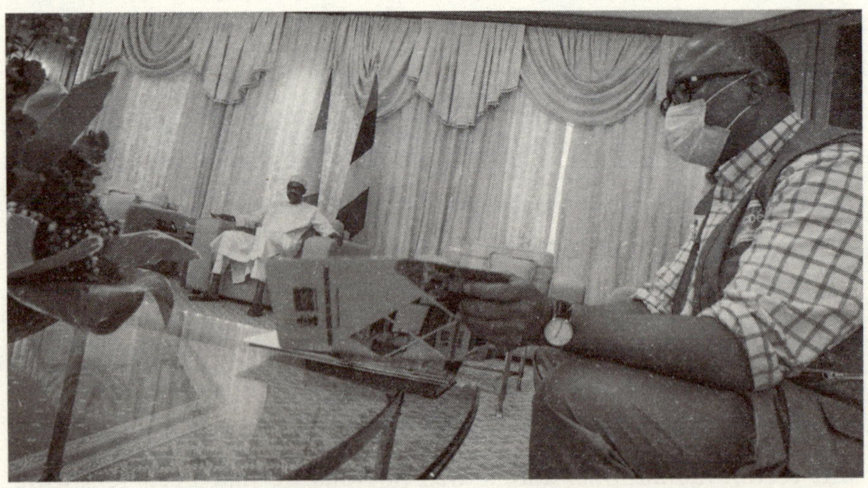

Figure 15: Briefing Mr President at his residence
Photo credit: Bayo Omoboriowo.

11

THE SCIENCE OF COMMUNICATION AND TRUST

April 2020

Day 39/Case 249

Two months before the world ever heard of the novel coronavirus, a simulation exercise called *Event 201* was organised by the World Economic Forum; the Gates Foundation; and Johns Hopkins Centre for Health Security. That October, a group of scientists were brought together to simulate a potential pandemic response based on different possibilities, providing answers to what we would do if certain scenarios emerged. This exercise would later become a talking point for conspiracy theorists and sceptics, who claimed that it was a rehearsal for the COVID-19 pandemic.

Simulation exercises, as we have seen, are common in public health practice. They are crucial to testing preparedness efforts and brainstorming decisions that leaders could potentially make in real-life situations. I'm certain that participants of the simulation exercise in October 2019 would have thought that a pandemic was at best, a distant possibility—something that may happen in the future but unlikely in our lifetimes and certainly not imminent. Nothing could have prepared us for what was to come, not even a well-planned simulation exercise.

As someone who had been studying the possibility of a pandemic for years, it was often frustrating to see how little people seemed to appreciate the threat of emerging infections, especially political leaders. To communicate this threat, I had used the famous TIME magazine cover that predicted the next pandemic in many of my presentations. I also shared the narrative of the AIDS pandemic and how it evolved, as well as the consequences of previous influenza pandemics. Communicating the threat of emerging infectious diseases was a particularly complex challenge, given that this threat wasn't immediately visible. I'm not sure I ever truly convinced anyone that a pandemic was a real possibility in our lifetime, yet here we were. Likewise, I always championed the importance of open, honest communication in the event of an outbreak.

Experience taught me the importance of clear communication in any outbreak response, a trait lacking in most government agencies in Nigeria. As the pandemic spread, we had to be upfront about our assessment of the situation and aim for clarity in the advice we provided. This wouldn't be easy to achieve amidst so much uncertainty, but as leader of NCDC, I considered communicating with the Nigerian public a sacred responsibility. If the people had adequate understanding of the situation, they would be motivated to support the response, and this will save lives.

Years before the COVID-19 pandemic, one of my major priorities was to build an effective communication team at NCDC—which appeared to be a nearly impossible mission in the beginning. Our civil service cadre didn't include communication officers or specialists. It was expected that the Ministry of Information would deploy their staff to other ministries and parastatals to perform this function. The colleague deployed to NCDC was an enthusiastic guy, but ill-equipped for the 24/7 news cycle of the 21st century. I was determined to build a strong communications team and considered effective communication crucial to our success in preventing and controlling disease outbreaks.

For five years, we tried various innovative approaches to building a communications team. We scouted talented individuals within the agency who had a passion for communication and trained them. We collaborated with other government agencies and civil society organisations to share knowledge and resources. And we sought support from international partners who had experience in building effective communication teams, even enlisting consultants from the private sector. Eventually, we built a team of mostly young colleagues, who rose to the challenge and excelled in the art of communicating with Nigerians.

Perhaps the most important thing we did before 2020 was identifying and training a group of NCDC leaders to act as spokespersons for the agency. This meant that the Director General didn't have to attend every single media briefing or be the only spokesperson for the agency. With several requests coming in daily, having a team of trained spokespersons was essential in ensuring that we could effectively communicate with the public and the media.

The results spoke for themselves. Our communication team played a critical role in keeping Nigerians informed and empowered during the pandemic. On the night that the first COVID-19 case was confirmed, the number of followers on our Twitter and Facebook platforms increased five-fold, reaching over one million followers in a month. While this increase in followers was a positive sign, it also came with its challenges. We were overwhelmed with requests for information on how to get tested and criticisms of our work—NCDC was blamed for almost everything that was wrong with Nigeria at the time. Notwithstanding, our communications team remained undaunted in supplying the information needed by the public.

We launched the NCDC Connect Centre in 2017, thanks to a US CDC grant. The objective of the centre was to serve as a public platform for information sharing, and to perhaps support the occasional outbreak response. The centre was also designed to coordinate our event-based surveillance; we mined information on infectious diseases and public health events from social and traditional media platforms on a daily basis, identifying rumours and escalating significant ones to State Epidemiologists for verification. In the beginning, we received very few calls; the team comprised only five employees that operated during normal working hours. We would receive an average of ten calls a day, including a few prank calls.

When the pandemic hit, things changed. Our call rate rocketed to at least 1,000 per day, and it became difficult to reach the call centre. While most calls were from people with genuine concerns and requests, we also received calls from people with complaints about things unrelated to the outbreak. Some called asking for financial support. Others called to check that the lines were working. Our once nearly idle call centre became one of the most challenging aspects of the pandemic response. It was our frontline in the fight against the virus, and as the pandemic progressed, five people could no longer handle the volume of calls we were receiving. We had to engage ad hoc staff, which meant training people within the shortest available time.

On few occasions, people received unclear information from our call agents, owing to lack of in-depth onboarding. Some of these calls were recorded and shared widely on social media, to discredit the agency. For each of these errors, we had thousands of successful calls that never made the headlines. But those erroneous messages hurt our credibility, and we had to work hard to regain the trust of the public. At the end of every week, we reviewed thousands of recorded calls to identify mistakes and re-train staff who were already working exceptionally long hours. I redeployed a senior colleague from our Surveillance department, Dr Muntari Hassan, to manage the connect centre on a full-time basis. The more calls we took, the more we learnt and improved our correspondence with the public, earning us the support of major telecommunications companies in Nigeria.

Figure 16: At the daily press briefing early in 2020
Photo credit: Ifeoluwa Ojo/IKP Studios

NCDC faced more cynicism from the public as the virus continued to spread. There were misunderstandings about where our responsibility started and ended, and we were criticised for actions outside our jurisdiction. Rumours and misinformation spread almost as fast as the virus itself. One day, a man called the connect centre to ask for help with transporting his sick father to the hospital. He didn't have a car and his father's condition was worsening. Our agent listened and empathised but explained that NCDC didn't have the resources to provide ambulance services and provided him with the number to call in his state. The man became terribly upset, shouting at the agent and accusing NCDC of not caring about people's lives. However, this wasn't an area where we could realistically intervene—we simply didn't have ambulances on ground in the states. This responsibility belonged to the state governments, but it was hard to explain.

On the Saturday afternoon after the first case was confirmed, our young communications team of less than ten people, along with partners in the area, met to form a broader crisis communication team, including heads of other response pillars. At this point, we were already overwhelmed and a major priority for me was to sustain the team's enthusiasm. They had received incessant criticism despite their hard work, and it was time to re-strategise. We reflected on recent challenges and opportunities. Many of the challenges were beyond our control, but we couldn't just ignore them. We also recognised that elevated mistrust among the population was affecting our ability to communicate. Therefore, one of our major priorities was to develop a strategy that wouldn't only rely on information transmitted to the population—but one that included the people and gave them a role to play. For instance, many Nigerians were calling for the international borders to be closed, but we knew that simply shutting down borders wouldn't be enough. If COVID-19 spread in our country, the responsibility would ultimately fall on the government, but citizens also had a role to play in preventing its spread.

As I sat in the Situation Room of the NCDC headquarters with the crisis communications team, the weight of the pandemic response was heavy on my shoulders. The demands being placed on our young and small communications team were overwhelming. Fortunately, Vivianne leads Nigeria Health Watch—a well-established health communication and advocacy organisation, and offered to lend her expertise. She also supported us with two other members of her team to work full-time with NCDC Crisis Communications Team. Prior to this, she had assisted in developing the initial guidelines of preventative measures for businesses and schools. Two other colleagues joined this team from partner organisations: Ukwori Ejibe from the Tony Blair Institute and Chijioke Kaduru from Corona Management Systems.

We knew that the responsibility of limiting the spread of COVID-19 wasn't the sole responsibility of the government, but how could we effectively communicate this message to the Nigerian people and encourage individuals to take responsibility for their actions? We wanted to tap into the community spirit of Nigerians, reminding people that we are in this together. During one of the daily press briefings by WHO, Dr Mike Ryan had repeatedly highlighted this sentiment, stating that citizens had a responsibility to play in the COVID-19 response. His words struck a chord, and as we brainstormed ideas, the #TakeResponsibility campaign was born—a campaign that would completely revitalise our communications efforts and inspire the masses to protect themselves and their communities. We were determined to make it a success.

Figure 17: A meeting with NCDC Crisis Communications team. Photo credit: Ifeoluwa Ojo/IKP Studios

The #TakeResponsibility campaign was designed to promote individual behavioural change by emphasising the role of individuals in safeguarding themselves and their loved ones, and highlighting the potential consequences of non-compliance. This placed the responsibility of individuals and self-organised groups at the fore of the accountability framework for decision-making. At the campaign launch, we established six critical messages that served as a rallying call for all Nigerians. We immediately began developing tools to support implementation, including graphics, jingles, social media messages and other materials to support the campaign. We sought help from UNICEF, Breakthrough Action Nigeria, and Centre for Communication and Social Impact (CCSI) to supplement our efforts.

The campaign continued to gain momentum, culminating in the successful adaptation of #CelebrateResponsibly during the Christmas and Salah holidays. As we continued to roll out our campaign messages, we received more support from various sectors. A notable supporter was Dettol Nigeria; they developed one of the first public adverts on COVID-19. They engaged popular Nigerian actress, Funke Akindele, who had previously done campaigns for Dettol to film an awareness video. We were grateful for their support, especially because we needed to convince several Nigerians that COVID-19 could affect anyone, regardless of economic status. We believed that Funke Akindele could help us reach a wider audience.

In April, a few weeks after the jingle started to air, and within a few days after the country had gone into lockdown, videos emerged on social media showing that Funke Akindele had hosted a party at her home, despite the physical distancing requirements by NCDC. We received numerous messages and could barely keep up with our Twitter mentions, text messages, and calls to the centre. The public accused NCDC of 'choosing' an ambassador who didn't follow the rules. This undermined our public campaign and resulted in more distrust. I was initially hesitant about responding to the public backlash as it distracted us from our objectives, but we stopped sharing the campaign video on our social media. Representatives from Dettol, with whom we had a good relationship, put out a statement clarifying that Ms Akindele was never an 'NCDC Ambassador' but was contracted by Dettol. After a few weeks, the backlash fizzled out, but we had lost progress through this incident. We, however, learnt a valuable lesson about the potential challenges of using brand ambassadors for public health campaigns.

Our communication campaign also received invaluable support from civil society organisations and leaders, including Innocent Chukwuma, the then West Africa Director for the Ford Foundation, and Atedo Peterside of the ANAP Foundation. They helped bring together other civil society and private sector leaders into a small group, led by Innocent, to champion our #TakeResponsibility campaign messages. Every Sunday, they convened virtually, and provided us with critical feedback on the COVID-19 response, including pointing out where we had gone wrong and offering recommendations for improvement.

The support they provided was especially important given that there were often aspects of the response that I, as a government official, couldn't publicly critique. For example, even after the incident with Funke Akindele, some politicians continued to host large events with no repercussions. This gave the impression that there was one rule for the elite and politicians, and another for ordinary Nigerians, making enforcement of the COVID-19 protocols much harder.

Innocent Chukwuma sadly passed away in April 2021, but his legacy lives on through his contributions to the COVID-19 response in Nigeria. I'm deeply grateful for the role played by Innocent and others like him. He was an incredibly patriotic Nigerian who led a team that was deeply committed to supporting the response in any way they could. We must continue to tell this story and push for a better public health system in Nigeria, in memory of Innocent and others who passed away during the COVID-19 response.

In addition to the efforts made by Innocent's team, a group of well-meaning people, some of whom I knew personally, formed a WhatsApp group to create graphics and messages which they shared for our review and disseminated widely through their personal platforms. They urged celebrities to partake in this campaign, with actress, Toyin Abraham, being one of the notable advocates who shared these messages in both English and Yoruba. It wasn't until 2022 that I discovered my successor at NCDC, Ifedayo Adetifa, was part of this small group of supporters. Popular Nigerian rapper, Ruggedman, contacted my team via Twitter to create free videos promoting COVID-19 preventive measures, which he shared on his Instagram page.

Before the pandemic, my team had attempted to get the NCDC Twitter account verified for four years, but we only received automated responses. I always believed that more could be done with Twitter and Facebook, given their vast reach in Nigeria. In 2017, we held a workshop with Facebook to discuss how we could maximise their platform to share public health messages, which resulted in ad credits for our meningitis and Lassa fever campaigns; they also helped in establishing a WhatsApp account for NCDC. We utilised the WhatsApp account to share information on the number of cases, testing locations, and to address general inquiries. When the first COVID-19 case was confirmed in Nigeria, Twitter representatives reached out to verify both NCDC and my personal account, which I used in my role as DG. Twitter also created a mechanism to ensure that NCDC account became the primary source of information for searches about COVID-19 on Nigerian Twitter. We eventually opened a Telegram account to ensure we reached as many Nigerians as possible.

To fully appreciate our COVID-19 communication strategy, we must acknowledge the indispensable role of traditional media—television, radio, and print. We received daily requests for interviews, a significant shift from 2016 and 2017 when we had to seek out television stations to share information about NCDC's work. Media organisations provided us with free or reduced airtime costs, and they shared our in-house produced jingles. NCDC staff appeared on various TV channels across the country, with some interviews conducted in local languages. These interviews were occasionally difficult, but we remained committed to leveraging traditional media to convey evidence-based information.

The establishment of the PTF on COVID-19 necessitated a 'whole-of-government' response approach, which was crucial for ensuring Federal Government alignment and cohesion. However, this approach posed risks to NCDC as we became the subject of criticisms for *all* government decisions, whether health or non-health related, within or outside our mandate. We were unjustly accused of mismanaging palliatives intended as social safety nets and inflating the number of cases to access donor funds, among other baseless allegations.

Consequently, we had to increase our security at the office and remove NCDC licence plates on our official vehicles. Our staff were subjected to insults and death threats on social media, and one incident involved a popular Instagram skit maker, Sydney Talker, who created a viral video claiming he was sick and couldn't get tested. This attracted threats from his fans, who wrongly assumed that NCDC staff were responsible for his inability to get tested. Some staff were afraid of returning home late at night due to threats from those who believed the COVID-19 pandemic came with extra financial benefits. On social media, every post was met with unfounded accusations and a distracting 'follow for follow' trend, prompting us to disable replies when sharing the daily number of confirmed COVID-19 cases.

The crisis communications team remained committed to providing consistent information about the pandemic, meticulously reviewing data on a weekly basis, including phone calls to NCDC Call Centre, conversations on our social media platforms, and insights from Health Promoters working in Ministries of Health across Nigeria's 36 states. Our small team developed weekly messaging priorities, based on data collected from NCDC rumour management system, social media platforms, and call centre amongst others. The messaging priorities were disseminated to the health promotion officers at the state level and translated into different communication tools such as infographics, short videos, skits, animation, newspaper cartoons and editorials.

We utilised every available channel to disseminate our messages, including partnering with respectable social media influencers at the onset of the pandemic. We also shared our messaging priorities with all Ministries, Departments, and Agencies to ensure alignment and cohesion in our efforts to keep Nigerians informed. In the age of social media, misinformation is a global phenomenon, often faceless and anonymous. The pandemic showed that the only way to combat misinformation was to build trust and confront it head-on, upholding the truth at all times.

12

PUBLIC-PRIVATE ALLIANCES

April 2020

Day 52/Case 641

Partnerships are the lifeblood of public health action. Successful ones are creative, dynamic associations that compensate for the shortfalls caused by insufficient funding for public health. Typically, non-governmental organisations form the majority of the partners in public health, but in most countries, the private sector also plays a major role in providing healthcare.

In the aftermath of the Ebola outbreak, Dr Ritgak Tilley-Gyado, who was working as an aide to the Minister of Health, wrote a fascinating report on the economic impact of the outbreak and the role of the private sector. This work shaped my thinking and influenced my decision to reach out to select businesses in the country. Ritgak's report laid out in unflinching terms, the possible dire consequences in the event of future epidemics but also advocated for the role of the private sector in mitigation.

In the years leading up to the pandemic, I had countless meetings and presentations with private sector leaders in Nigeria, hoping to encourage support in NCDC. This was spurred by the devastating Ebola outbreak in 2014, believing that lessons had been learnt, and the people would be convinced of the importance of investing in pandemic preparedness. In these meetings, I presented facts and figures of the potential impact of an infectious disease outbreak on their businesses and urged them to consider investing in pandemic preparedness. I used Dr Ritgak's report to make a case for their increased involvement in epidemic preparedness in Nigeria. The reps would nod politely and thank me for the presentation, but as soon as the meeting was over, they rushed off to their next appointments without so much as a backward glance. Little did we know that a pandemic was just around the corner.

In 2018, I was privileged to visit the CDC Foundation in Atlanta with my colleague and Senior Epidemiologist, Dr Fatima Saleh. During our visit, we met with Dr Judy Monroe and her team. She explained the role that the foundation, which she led, played in public health delivery, especially focusing on their work with private sector entities in the US. We discussed a potential collaboration, and I shared our vision of engaging Nigeria's private sector in our work. I learnt a lot from this mission and went back to Nigeria re-energised.

Later that year, I found a valuable partner in my friend Dr Muntaqa Umar-Sadiq, the Chief Executive Officer of the Private Sector Healthcare Alliance of Nigeria (PSHAN). When I laid out my plans, his interest was immediate. We brainstormed strategic ways to create a framework for engaging the private sector in epidemic preparedness and response efforts in Nigeria, a cause that was aligned with the organisation he led. We decided to form an organisation much like the CDC Foundation in the US and named it the Alliance for Epidemic Preparedness and Response (A4EPR). Our vision was to create a platform to engage with the private sector in a way that would inspire confidence in its fiduciary functions. I knew that for many private entities in Nigeria, direct funding to government agencies wasn't an appealing proposition.

Creating the A4EPR was no easy task. Despite other responsibilities, Dr Umar-Sadiq and I fully committed to its launch. We organised concept notes, presentations, conducted research into areas of interest, and more. We believed in our vision, and we felt this organisation could be a game-changer in Nigeria's fight against infectious diseases, as well as a great partner to NCDC. I had big dreams of how responsible collaboration would lead to benefits for all involved. After obtaining all the necessary paperwork, we geared up for a series of meetings with major corporations in Nigeria to share our vision. Together with Ukwori Ejibe—an embedded staff of one of our partners—the Tony Blair Institute, and the PSHAN team, we made calls and secured appointments. We persisted through multiple rejections and eventually landed a few meetings.

On a particular trip to Lagos to meet some of our prospective partners, a major oil firm in Nigeria, was our third stop of the day, and it turned out to be quite the adventure. We waited outside the premises in the pouring rain. When we were allowed in, we were totally drenched, and to our surprise, we weren't taken to the office of the corporate leadership but to the clinic, where we managed a fruitful discussion with the Medical Director, sharing our vision for A4EPR and the importance of private sector engagement in health security. Unfortunately, but perhaps not surprisingly, we left with no commitment and little hope.

Regardless of these setbacks, our undeterred team worked diligently to organise the launch event. On the D-day, we were pleased to have both the Minister of Health and the Minister of State for Health in attendance. However, to our disappointment, we were unable to convince a single Chief Executive from the corporate sector to join us for the event. It was disheartening. At the end of the day, no commitments were made. Amid our frustration, we realised that raising funds for epidemics during peacetime was going to be an uphill battle. But we never gave up.

The pandemic flipped the switch. Everyone suddenly realised the severity of the situation. Companies called us to inquire about staff evacuations and risk mitigation strategies. The organisation that kept us in the rain, was one of the first companies to contact us for assistance when cases began to emerge among their employees. Some people even resorted to calling Vivianne, who had to filter the messages to me.

To further manage the flood of requests, I set up a dedicated team to provide structured advice to large private corporations. After discussing with Dr Sani Aliyu in his capacity as coordinator of the PTF, we decided to encourage major private sector enterprises to form a single entity to support the response. Zouera Youssoufou of the *Dangote Foundation* already had a similar idea, and in no time, a coalition emerged. Nigeria's largest conglomerates came together to form the Coalition Against COVID-19 (CACOVID), pooling their resources to provide technical and operational support, and aggressive advocacy of the government's response to the outbreak.

CACOVID became an integral part of the country's response against the escalating pandemic. Corporate Nigeria managed to come together in support of the country without overburdening the already stretched-to-the-limit primary responders. The coalition's steering committee comprised committed professionals from key conglomerates, which ensured that their interventions were well-coordinated and aligned with the national response plan. Some of the most significant interventions by CACOVID were the direct provision of infrastructure, equipment, and reagents to support the response. For some of these interventions, they requested guidance from NCDC, and for others, they proceeded on their own.

One area CACOVID prioritised without guidance from NCDC was the construction of temporary isolation centres across the country. This initiative must have been driven by similar efforts around the world, displayed on our television screens. At first, the idea of building temporary centres as had been done in China and a few other countries seemed sound, but it soon became obvious that this would require more than constructing physical structures. We needed to ensure the centres had access to essential amenities such as electricity, sanitation, security, and food. Unfortunately, planning and coordination have never been areas of strength in Nigeria, and this situation was no exception. As a result, many isolation centres set up across the country never served their intended purpose, resulting in a huge waste of resources at a time of great scarcity.

We made progress in the procurement of laboratory reagents. CACOVID engaged with us to understand the needs of the laboratory sector, and once we provided them with a detailed description of the required reagents, commodities, and equipment, they handled the procurement process directly. Throughout the pandemic, they delivered these items to us at regular intervals. It was a huge success and a testament to what can be achieved when different sectors come together to tackle a common problem.

The coalition also supported the response in many ways not immediately obvious to casual observers. Early in the response, they mobilised artists and prominent Nigerians to use their platforms to encourage adherence to NCDC guidelines. This helped raise awareness about the pandemic and promote appropriate behaviour to reduce the risk of getting infected. They provided critical social support to millions of Nigerians who were unable to work due to the pandemic, creating a necessary safety net in a country where such programs were lacking. Sadly, the distribution of items such as food supplements was hampered by logistical challenges in some states, and the items were left unused in warehouses.

The development and management of the Nigeria International Travel Portal (NITP) was another remarkable achievement that wouldn't have been possible without the support of the private sector. In response to the economic impact of the pandemic on commercial flights, the PTF developed recommendations for the resumption of international travel. However, the high number of COVID-19 cases being recorded in countries like the US and the UK—popular travel destinations for Nigerians—meant that we had to be careful.

The NITP was one of the first travel portals in the world, designed to manage international travel traffic during the pandemic. We needed a system that could ensure travellers were tested before arriving in the country, isolated upon arrival, and tested again after entry. The platform also had to provide us with data to track the contacts of identified cases, which would require careful regulatory and payment considerations. To achieve this, we convened an extraordinary group of Nigerian leaders, including Herbert Wigwe of Access Bank, Segun Agbaje of Guaranty Trust Bank, and Zouera Youssoufou of the Dangote Foundation. These leaders and their teams brought their expertise and resources to the table, working together with us at NCDC and PTF to develop and operationalise the NITP. We were fortunate to have the technical support of colleagues such as Lawal Bakare, who had previously collaborated with me in 2016 on developing NCDC's communication and branding strategies. Lawal's expertise in developing digital tools for outbreak response was invaluable to our efforts during the pandemic.

The rapid development and deployment of NITP came with challenges and risks. While NCDC was already hosting an array of digital services, it had never hosted a platform that would generate that amount of daily traffic all year round. The poor digitisation of government services in Nigeria means that each government institution is responsible for its own websites and other digital tools. As with any large IT project, technical issues cropped up along the way, and we were vigilant, working quickly to resolve each problem and prevent recurrence. In hindsight, I wish we had more time to develop and test various options before implementing them. But given the urgency of the situation, we had no such luxury. Hosting the platform also meant that we had to take full ownership of it, especially in the eyes of the public, and deal with criticism associated with hurriedly launching an online platform expected to function perfectly all the time. We publicly apologised for major glitches and worked to improve the system, making the travel portal a valuable resource that supported international travel in Nigeria.

We had to navigate the complexities of reaching agreements with each state government and establishing private laboratories within states to conduct testing on arrival. Every state had varying capacities to carry out testing and limited resources. We overcame these hurdles by engaging with state governments and private sector partners to ensure the successful implementation of the portal. To support their response, each state was allowed to keep a portion of the costs from the travel tests. This didn't mean, as it later came to be believed by some Nigerians, that NCDC was making money from this portal. Absolutely none of the funds generated through travel-related testing came to NCDC.

The success of the NITP led to restored faith in the system. Many countries around the world subsequently attempted to develop portals to support the restoration of travel, and we were pleased to be pioneers. The rapid development and deployment of NITP attested to the power of collaboration and the critical role of the private sector in meeting public sector priorities.

During the early stages of the pandemic, diagnostic reagents were in short supply worldwide. One Saturday, I received multiple requests for reagents from laboratories, and our regular suppliers were running low on stock. My instincts told me that we could find what we needed in Nigeria, but due to market failures—all too common in the country—the supplies weren't easy to locate. I took a different approach by tweeting from my verified handle, asking potential suppliers to reach out to me directly. I knew this was an unusual way to source supplies, but I was more focused on getting what we needed. As expected, the tweet was met with backlash and criticism, but I remained unfazed. Within a few hours, a supplier called me from Abuja, offering to supply the reagents we needed. He even suggested we finalised the paperwork by Monday. This was his way of supporting the response, and it was heart-warming to see the power of leveraging different networks to achieve our goals during the acute phase of the response.

Later, I considered a tough decision that would either make or break our response efforts. To scale up our capacity, we had to include private laboratories in the country's testing efforts. Various stakeholders resisted and criticised this move, but we had to ramp up our testing capacity as the pandemic showed no signs of slowing down. Bringing private laboratories on board wasn't a straightforward process. We had to ensure that strict quality standards and testing protocols were adhered to. This involved a structured process of inspection, accreditation, and certification. As we began this process, we encountered pressure from various regulatory authorities and unions, who wanted to be involved in the response efforts. While some had genuine passion for service, I suspected that there were vested interests at play.

We carried out strict inspections to ensure that all biosafety cabinets and equipment were in place before accreditation. This took time, but there was no room for error, and we weren't going to take any shortcuts. While we faced criticism from private lab owners who felt we were taking too long to get them accredited, we were determined to maintain quality standards. Through this, NCDC was developing a reputation of being thorough and unwilling to bend the rules; I was most proud. We successfully onboarded many private laboratories, which boosted our testing capacity. I learnt the importance of taking calculated risks and being open to unconventional solutions in times of crisis.

Throughout this process, we had the support of Dhamari Naidoo, a WHO laboratory specialist who had also worked with me during the 2014 Ebola outbreak. She had been working in the WHO Country Office for over a year before the pandemic started. She provided invaluable support in translating WHO's global guidance to our national context across several areas, including testing, quality control, and more. Her expertise was a tremendous asset to us during this challenging time and provided just the type of support we needed from WHO.

We also received support from private companies and religious organisations. *God is Good Motors,* the popular Nigerian logistics company, connected with us on Twitter, and provided us with four buses and drivers, free-of-charge. This enabled our staff commute to and from work during the lockdown when there was no public transportation available. We also received support from banks and mobile phone companies, which helped us expand our call centres. Supermarkets and restaurants sent us drinks and food. I remember one Saturday after a particularly tough week when we heard that an Abuja school had organised a food fair and sent cookies, cakes, and other desserts for our staff. This lifted our spirts—seriously, we didn't take any support for granted.

Nigerians in the diaspora organised themselves into groups to support the response. It was overwhelming receiving such generous donations from people who were also affected by the pandemic. We documented every single donation we received, big or small, for posterity. We uploaded this information on the NCDC website, so that everyone could see the incredible support we received. These gestures of kindness and generosity gave us strength and motivation to continue our work in spite of enormous challenges.

The COVID-19 pandemic has left an indelible mark on our nation and highlighted the critical need for government and private sector collaboration in responding to crises. We have learnt valuable lessons on how to achieve better results in terms of sustainability and resilience, and must build on these lessons for future outbreaks in Nigeria. By doing so, we can build a more resilient and sustainable healthcare system that benefits all Nigerians. I sincerely hope we wouldn't need another crisis to realise the importance of a strong partnership between NCDC and the private sector in Nigeria.

13

WITHIN STATE BORDERS

April–May 2020

Day 61/Case 1,932

Nigeria operates a federal system of government, with the central power radiating to the different levels of governance. This federal system has far-reaching implications on almost everything we do in the country, and the health sector is no exception. The constitution is largely quiet in defining the scope of healthcare delivery at the different tiers of government, leading to confusion within and beyond the health sector. This lack of clarity was either not apparent to everyone or it was often ignored. In public discourses, people state their expectations of what 'government' should do; however, it was not clear to them and everyone else in this discourse, which part of government they are referring to.

The response to the COVID-19 outbreak in Nigeria further exposed some of the unique challenges of our federal system of governance in terms of responsibilities for outbreak prevention, detection, and response. In any large response to an emergency, a specified command-and-control boosts efficiency, but this wasn't the case in Nigeria. In the absence of a more unified governance structure, we had to operate within state borders, while coordinating national level activities.

Early in the response, I attended regular PTF meetings where we deliberated the best way to approach the COVID-19 outbreak. One of the hardest decisions we made was recommending that the President impose a ban on travel between states. We considered it a necessary measure to limit the spread of the virus, and advised that the travel ban began with three states: Lagos, Ogun, and the Federal Capital Territory. Eventually, the ban would be extended to all states. Lagos and the FCT were the major points of entry into the country, accounting for most of the early cases. Lagos in particular housed Nigeria's busiest international airport, hosting 70% of international air travel. Ogun surrounds Lagos State, making it impossible to practically separate it, yet some argued that including Ogun wasn't necessary since it had relatively few cases at the time. After intense consultation within the PTF, which included the Ministers of Aviation and Interior, we all agreed that it was a necessary step. On March 18, we advised Mr President to approve the restriction of movement into and out of these three states.

The decision was scrutinised by the public and soon accepted as the right thing to do. The travel ban marked the beginning of intense discussions with state governments about all aspects of the response—primarily focused on finding the balance between 'lives and livelihood.' After the PTF was established, we realised that close coordination was needed with state governors across the country. Thankfully, the Vice President, Professor Yemi Osinbajo, who was also the Chairman of the National Economic Council (NEC), formed a subcommittee of governors to align efforts and serve as the primary engagement counterpart for the PTF. This subcommittee comprised the Governors of Plateau, Anambra, Lagos, Kaduna, Bauchi, and Ogun, as well as the Minister for the FCT—chaired by the Governor of Delta State, Ifeanyi Okowa.

Governor Okowa took his role seriously. The meetings were punctual, engaging, and well-managed by the NEC Secretariat. As is the norm in Nigeria, every meeting began and ended with prayers, alternating between the dominant Muslim and Christian faiths. There was some banter, but for most of it, we had serious, often tense conversations. The committee addressed the difficulties of implementing certain measures, especially the closure of places of worship and markets. We discussed resource allocation to states to alleviate the impact of restrictions and subsequent security implications. Through these gatherings, we attempted to harmonise policies between federal and state levels, developing a coherent narrative of our response to maintain the trust of the Nigerian people. Dr Okowa and I provided monthly reports to the NEC.

Figure 18: Briefing Mr Vice President during the National Economic Council Meeting. Photo credit: Ifeoluwa Ojo/IKP Studios

Working with Mr Vice President was a real pleasure. He was always courteous, expressing his gratitude for our efforts and encouraging us to do more. Despite disagreements that arose during the NEC meetings, he managed the governors with grace and confidence, never losing his cool even in the face of antagonism. Achieving full alignment with all of Nigeria's states was never going to be easy. Some states initially disagreed with the national response approach, especially our strategy of aggressive testing and case isolation, which formed the basis of our early control strategy. Cross River State, for instance, declined implementing the national response strategy of testing all suspected COVID cases, claiming that our tests weren't effective. A Cross River State Commissioner even criticised our work on national television. The disagreement often got so heated that it affected healthcare workers in the state.

The University of Calabar Teaching Hospital, managed by the Federal Government, was caught between following the guidance of NCDC and pandering to the state government. The absurdity of the situation was captured by the case of a UN employee based in Cross River, who fell critically ill with suspected COVID-19 symptoms. He had to be smuggled out of the state for testing and treatment, and tested positive for COVID in a neighbouring state where he underwent treatment; despite the state insisting it didn't have any COVID cases. The Governor of Cross River State accused NCDC leadership of blindly following 'Western' approaches for diagnosis and treatment. He asserted that his scientific background afforded him greater insight into how to manage the situation. Our team refused to be deterred by the criticism and continued to focus on evidence-based responses. Through several adversarial public pronouncements by the Cross River State government, we kept our cool and provided the necessary advice and support.

After the Federal Government eased interstate travel, the Cross River government implemented its own strategy, closing off its borders, with the Governor often sitting at the border posts himself and sharing this with the media. This caused incredible hardship to travellers, who ended up in tailbacks on roads leading to the state. The media immediately picked up on this, highlighting areas of misalignment between the national and state responses in a few states.

Eventually, interstate travel restrictions were lifted, and testing was finally allowed in Cross River. Our colleagues and the public health workers in Cross River State were finally allowed to do their jobs and engage the national response. We were able to provide enthusiastic support to the state and repaired relationships that were strained during the earlier stages of the outbreak. Unsurprisingly, cases were quickly identified, but it was blamed on the influx of people from outside the state, given its 'successful response.'

In contrast, the conflict with Kogi State was never resolved. Despite bordering with nine other states and being an important thoroughfare, the Governor declared Kogi 'COVID-free' from the beginning of the response and went as far as denying the existence of the virus. We tried everything to persuade him to support the national response, but all our attempts fell on deaf ears. He never wore face masks, except when he had to meet Mr President.

The NCDC team sent to support the state's response was 'deported' on arrival by the Governor himself—on live television! They were accused of shaking hands with the welcoming team without gloves, thereby breaking 'NCDC protocols' and given the option of either going into quarantine for two weeks or being taken back to Abuja. The team chose to leave and was escorted by the Governor's security team to the border between Kogi and the FCT. I couldn't sleep that night until they were safely in their homes in Abuja.

During a conversation with a national news outlet, the interviewer was persistent on engaging me in a direct confrontation with the Governor of Kogi State, and I refused to take the bait. As the head of a Federal Government agency, I understood that our primary responsibility was to support state governments in their roles. For us to do this, the state governments must be receptive. Governors wield enormous power in Nigeria, and as such, it wasn't in my best interest to confront any governor directly. I made it clear that if a state government refused our offer of assistance, it wasn't my responsibility to insist on providing support. During the interview, which was broadcast live to the entire country, I emphasised that it was up to the citizens of each state to elect the leadership they wanted. If a state government chose to expel Federal Government agencies, then so be it. My job was to ensure that we provided the necessary support to those who welcomed it, and to maintain a level-headed approach in the face of adversity.

After the interview, I received messages of support from Nigerians across the country; it was gladdening to find that many people shared our view on the situation, including colleagues in Kogi State. Many were afraid to share this support publicly, and I understood. We continued to do our job to the best of our abilities, repairing relationships where possible, and supporting those who were receptive to our help. Fortunately, 35 out of 36 states in Nigeria were more than willing to collaborate with us and fight earnestly for our survival.

Another bone of contention was the disbursement of a World Bank facility to support state-level vaccination efforts, revealing yet another fault line in our federal structure. In Nigeria, most states have primary healthcare boards that oversee primary healthcare delivery, including immunisation. These boards work with the National Primary Healthcare Development Agency (NPHCDA). The Primary Healthcare Boards at the state level are generally led by an executive director and are often in conflict with the Commissioners of Health over the control of resources. In this case, the Commissioners were unhappy with the proposal that they wouldn't oversee the management of resources to support COVID vaccination efforts.

Generally, the pandemic highlighted challenges faced by federal agencies in reaching agreements with state levels on various aspects of the response. While some countries were successful in coordinating their response at the national level, others struggled with national-level coordination. The political decision-making process throughout the response in Nigeria and other federally governed countries received serious post-pandemic scrutiny. As the pandemic declined, a major concern was the state governments' capacity to sustain the considerable investment made in the public health infrastructure in their states. Unfortunately, at the time of writing this chapter, many states have reverted to the status quo, reinforcing the cycle of neglect. Many laboratories and treatment centres established at the peak of the pandemic are now closed or running at limited capacity due to inadequate funding from state governments.

14

PARTNERING WITH UN AGENCIES

May 2020

Day 76/Case 4,641

Working with the UN was a routine practice for NCDC, and the COVID-19 pandemic magnified the unique experience we had with them.

While the UN is often criticised for its bureaucracy and inefficiency—which holds some truth—our experience in Nigeria during the pandemic was different. We witnessed a significant shift in the UN's approach towards efficient and focused support to the Nigerian government, which played a crucial role in our response efforts. Over the years, I have learnt that the approach of UN agencies can vary greatly, depending on the leadership in place and the level of risk they are willing to take at any given time. But during the pandemic, we needed the support of leaders who were willing to take bold action and push beyond the norm.

At NCDC, we have always considered WHO our natural partner, but we collaborated with other UN entities like UNICEF, UNAIDS, UNDP and UNFPA. The resources and expertise available in these organisations have been an invaluable asset for our work, but it also led to an over-reliance on their assistance. In the early weeks of January, as the pandemic began to spread globally, Dr Sani Aliyu and I set out to get the most out of the various UN agencies in Nigeria, without abdicating our leadership roles to them. As experienced leaders in public health, we knew that time was of the essence, and we were eager to tap into the resources and expertise of the UN. We were both aware of the bureaucracy of the UN system and how long it can take to get any proposal approved. I doubted the UN's ability to provide speedy assistance. This wasn't the time for lengthy proposal developments and their preference for 'results framework with clear indicators, timelines, and deliverables.' We had to act fast.

On a Tuesday morning in March, I received a call from the country representative of the UNDP in Nigeria, Mohammed Yahya or 'Mo,' as we fondly called him. Mo became a friend and brother ever since we first met. He fully immersed himself in Nigeria, not only performing his duties but also trying to understand our people and culture. We had developed a unique bond, and I was grateful for it. When I answered the call, I was greeted with Mo's usual exuberance.

"Chikwe my brother, we have a plan!"

I was intrigued, but as always in those days, impatient. He informed me that he and a few other leaders in the UN, together with the representative of the European Union in Nigeria and some key partners, were setting up a 'UN Basket Fund.' The basket fund would pool resources from different UN agencies, as well as international partners, to support Nigeria's response to COVID-19. It was an exciting prospect. In addition to the potential for significant resources to support the response, it alleviated the burden of individually negotiating with all the agencies.

Mo wanted my support in joining the governance structure to help prioritise interventions and allocate funds. This was a new concept for me. In all my years as NCDC's Director General, I had never seen much sharing of funds among UN organisations, making this proposal quite unusual. What's more, the idea of asking us for our opinion on *how* to support our efforts and including us in the decision-making process was almost unheard of. It was refreshing to see such a collaborative approach being taken, and I knew this could be a game-changer for the pandemic response. After thanking Mo for his proposal, I agreed to work with the UN on this initiative.

The UN Basket Fund facilitated the direct purchase of essential commodities and funded priority interventions across the country. I was particularly pleased that Dr Sani Aliyu and I were involved in the governance of the project. We sat on the Project Board, which was responsible for making all relevant decisions. The UN Basket Fund eventually raised about 22 million US dollars, which directly addressed some of our most urgent needs. It pooled and unified governance of resources from various donors, significantly reducing fragmentation—especially in the acute phase of the pandemic—increasing the collective response to the pandemic, as well as collective responsibility and accountability. It was a true collaborative effort, which enabled relevant public sector leaders to direct resources toward interventions that maximised pandemic response, while also providing donors with opportunities to contribute their diverse expertise. A report on monies received and allocated through the Basket Fund was published on the UNDP Nigeria website. This level of transparency was essential in building trust with the public and ensuring accountability.

In Abuja, the UN set up a treatment centre. The United Nations Population Fund (UNFPA) Resident representative in Nigeria, Ulla

Müller, played a critical role in setting the centre up. We liaised over the phone, and she ensured the centre was adequately resourced. While the centre primarily served the UN community in Nigeria, it also provided vital services to members of the diplomatic community who had chosen to remain in Nigeria during the pandemic. It was important for us to build their confidence in our services to retain their presence. We provided them with our national guidelines, advice, and training and worked closely together. The majority of those treated at their facility were Nigerians and their families.

When I first began my role, I was concerned about the level of involvement of WHO and other UN agencies as well as development partners in the delivery of operations in the public health sector. They seemed to be doing so much for us, things that we should really be doing by ourselves. All this started long before the establishment of NCDC, when Nigeria lacked a robust national public health agency to respond to the many disease outbreaks, especially those occurring in conflict-affected areas.

Outbreak responses were mostly ad hoc, chaotic and uncoordinated, with associated risks. Unsurprisingly, one of these outbreaks had led to an international incident that brought the country a lot of disrepute and nearly jeopardised global polio eradication efforts. A large meningitis outbreak in Kano State in 1996 provided an opportunity for the pharmaceutical firm *Pfizer* to conduct a clinical trial in which 100 children were given an experimental oral antibiotic called *Trovan*. It was later established that all the necessary due processes were not followed, and questions were raised over the documentation of the trial. The case was later settled out of court but had a deep and lasting impact on the polio eradication programme in Nigeria, as well as trust in public health authorities.

After this incident and given the weak state of the public health systems in Nigeria, we had a dilemma. The world had committed to a global public health priority of eliminating polio, which depended on success in Nigeria. To achieve this, WHO developed a dedicated polio surveillance system including its own laboratories. Given the absence of a national public health agency at the time, the entire polio response effort was led by a sister agency, the National Primary Healthcare Development Agency, which was primarily responsible for immunisation services but not surveillance and outbreak response. The laboratories were hosted in the University of Ibadan and University of Maiduguri. This approach created a dependency on WHO for almost all aspects of outbreak response in Nigeria. While we made good progress towards polio elimination, I can't say the same for most other diseases.

However, given the pressing nature of some global health priorities, especially polio eradication, as well as the acknowledged inefficiencies of the Nigerian state in many areas, it often seemed easier for WHO to recruit their own staff and coordinate tasks that we should be handling by ourselves. WHO's ability to recruit the best people locally without depending on public sector salaries helped them attract individuals with unique skill sets and motivation.

Agencies of the Federal Government of Nigeria couldn't afford to pay people competitive salaries, so it was not surprising that our staff were less motivated, and things did not work as well when left in the hands of government. WHO itself was being funded by a large group of partners to deliver on this important global target of eradication for the world.

In summary, over many years, many important public health functions in Nigeria have been delivered by UN agencies and other partners. Nigeria is not the only country, nor is health the only sector where this happens. The niggling question on my mind was how we were ever going to learn to take responsibility for our own destiny, if international organisations were doing for us, the things that we should be doing for ourselves. Until today, most of the resources that are spent on important public health priorities such as immunisation, HIV/AIDS are delivered with donor funds and efforts.

Countries like India, Pakistan, and others where the urgency of achieving immediate global public health goals didn't always align with the development priorities of individual countries suffered this same fate, but they gradually took more control of their destiny. I was determined that our relationship with the UN bodies as an agency had to be well-delineated, especially considering historical antecedents, and will not be determined by near-term goals alone. But to achieve this, without compromising on the health of people would not be easy.

Before the pandemic, NCDC had established a strong relationship with all UN agencies, especially with WHO. In 2016, Dr Wondi Alemu was appointed as WHO's Nigeria Representative—WR as they are called. I had long admired his work in developing the Integrated Disease Surveillance and Response (IDSR) strategy for WHO's African regional office, and I considered him a visionary leader and valuable colleague. I anticipated that he would be a strong ally in achieving the 'integration' of our surveillance efforts. In addition to formal work meetings, we would meet outside of work, often for hours, and I would share my vision for NCDC and Nigeria. Dr Alemu was a wise and calm communicator who approached his work with confidence and an unconventional perspective. We developed a trusting relationship and were candid about the strengths and limitations of our organisations. We committed to supporting each other in the development of a strong national public health agency, with WHO as a confident partner by our sides, but never in front of us. Ultimately, we wanted the country to take charge of its public health efforts.

Under the leadership of Dr Alemu, we ensured WHO's resources were available to us for outbreak detection and response, emphasising the importance of the country leading the charge. He was comfortable with WHO being seen in support of Government and not acting in place of Government. Following Dr Alemu's tenure, we built a strong, mutually beneficial, and respectful relationship between WHO and NCDC. This included monthly joint standing meetings, hosting WHO officials at NCDC's EOC and vice versa.

In 2018, Dr Alemu surprised me with an unexpected proposal. The DG of WHO, Dr Tedros Ghebreyesus and his entire leadership team, as well as the regional Directors of all WHO regional offices, were holding their annual meeting in Abuja. He had decided to bring them to NCDC to show them the work WHO was doing in strengthening national institutions. After a week of intense planning, we put together a detailed programme highlighting the outcomes of good WHO/country collaboration. The visit was beyond successful. We were honoured to showcase our work and discuss our plans for the future with such a distinguished audience.

Figure 19: The DG of WHO Dr Tedros Ghebreyesus visits NCDC.
Photo credit: Tijesu Ojumu

This strong relationship between NCDC and WHO country office resulted in a mutually respectful working relationship in the early months of the pandemic. Dr Fiona Braka of WHO Country office in Nigeria accompanied me on my national tour of states, and we worked together seamlessly, reinforcing each other's position. The presence of WHO on our side further strengthened the governors' confidence in our recommendations. Additionally, they facilitated our access to critical supplies and equipment needed for the response and provided training to staff at NCDC and across different states. WHO supported us with logistics that allowed us effectively deploy response teams to multiple states. This was particularly beneficial in Lagos, where we had deployed teams for several months.

Peter Hawkins, the UNICEF Representative in Nigeria at the time, shared my vision of a robust country-led response and encouraged his team to work with us and through us, rather than operating independently or going directly to the field. Slowly, we were able to demonstrate our ability to lead and deliver for our people, and our partners adjusted to the reality that they were there to support, not lead.

Prior to the pandemic, we had a strong collaborative relationship with UNAIDS, which was more aligned with the National Agency for the Control of AIDS due to its specialisation. This relationship was strengthened when we worked together on the Nigeria HIV/AIDS Indicator and Impact Survey (NAIIS) a few years before the pandemic. Our national reference laboratory provided the central laboratory for the survey. Dr Erasmus Morah who led UNAIDS in Nigeria provided strong support for these efforts, becoming a close friend and brother. We would often have thought-provoking conversations, so I always designated enough time—at least an hour—to his calls. We engaged each other in lively debates and explored various options, but in the end, we almost always reached a consensus on the best way forward.

Erasmus' passion for Nigeria was admirable, and his vast experience in responding to the HIV/AIDs pandemic was a key strength. When he asked how UNAIDS could better support NCDC, I requested a highly skilled epidemiologist. Thus, Professor Ehi Igunmbor, a South African-trained epidemiologist, joined NCDC and quickly became an invaluable part of the response. He was at the heart of the agency's scientific work and spear-headed the implementation of the sero-surveys conducted in four states and published later in October. Professor Ehi's impact extended far beyond his technical expertise. He mentored and empowered many young epidemiologists, providing them with guidance and opportunities. Ehi's legacy lives on through the many NCDC staff members he trained and inspired.

Throughout the response, Erasmus continued to be a great source of support and camaraderie. He formed a small, informal support group of other trusted friends and colleagues. Together, we analysed events and trends related to the pandemic across the continent. Erasmus ensured that we were always cautious and informed about what other countries were doing to enable us stay ahead of the curve. This innovative approach, alongside the respectful conduct demonstrated by the UN during the COVID-19 response in Nigeria, exemplifies how crucial global entities can operate within countries.

15

THE CONSONANCE BETWEEN CLINICIANS AND ACADEMICS

October 2020

Day 197/Case 60, 430

The vacuum created by limited treatment and prevention options in the first year of the pandemic led to an influx of proposals from various sectors of society—both local and global.

Everyone, desperate to 'fix' the situation, seemed to have a groundbreaking, novel solution to offer. There were newfound cures with miraculous discovery stories. But the truth is, Alexander Fleming's story of the discovery of penicillin would be a rare phenomenon in this age. Most new medicines have moderate effects that are difficult to demonstrate. It takes years of trials, a lot of money and expertise, and sometimes a stroke of luck to prove that a treatment works. But the pressure inflicted by the pandemic—dying patients, stalled economies, and public panic—precipitated medical quackery that dominated global conversations and nearly derailed response efforts. At the frontline of these 'fixes', in our context in Nigeria, were three major culprits.

Culprit 1: Hydroxychloroquine

The hydroxychloroquine theory began in the US and Europe and can be traced back to previous pandemics. Initial studies appeared to show promising results in limiting the activity of the virus in laboratory settings, but before studies were completed, social media hijacked the story and propelled it into mainstream media. Soon, there was a global shortage of the drug, even in countries renowned for their highly educated populations and great scientists. I remember being questioned on why we weren't stockpiling the medication like other countries, with people saying things like, ". . . if they are doing it, why aren't you? Do they know something you don't?"

As a country with years of experience in using chloroquine to manage malaria, Nigeria wasn't immune to the hype. In fact, many prominent academics and thought leaders reached out to me, advising us to start producing and stockpiling hydroxychloroquine. The pressure to recommend hydroxychloroquine even came from colleagues who should have known better—I still have many of their WhatsApp messages. The pressure was intense, and it seemed that rational thought processes had been replaced by unchecked desperation. I resisted including hydroxychloroquine in our treatment guidelines, but this didn't stop many clinicians from prescribing it and consequently, the price for hydroxychloroquine skyrocketed. Even after WHO announced that there was enough data to show it was ineffective and could even cause harm, some colleagues insisted on continuing trials in Nigeria.

Culprit 2: The Madagascar Cure

When the pandemic showed no signs of abating, more 'solutions' emerged. The President of Madagascar claimed to have found a cure for COVID-19 and sent a sample to President Muhammadu Buhari. President Buhari dutifully announced that the substance would be sent to appropriate regulatory bodies for assessment. But the media frenzy had already started and pressure mounted. There was a strong emotional appeal of having an African-solution to the pandemic. Questions were being asked on why there were no local cures coming out of Nigeria as well. Suddenly, all sorts of remedies were being sent to us. The Chair of the Presidential Task Force directed that the National Institute for Pharmaceutical Research and Development (NIPRD) be primarily responsible for the evaluation of these local remedies. As expected, it was proven that the Madagascar Cure had no effect on the disease and its safety remained undetermined. Madagascar went on to have a surge of cases. There were media queries, but we remained steadfast in our commitment to science and refused to compromise on our standards.

Culprit 3: Zinc and Ivermectin

Zinc and ivermectin were two other medications of proven value for other conditions that enjoyed a lot of attention from clinicians in Nigeria. Although there was no evidence of efficacy in improving clinical outcomes for COVID for either medication, zinc had been used for a long time without causing harm, especially for pregnant women. Therefore, I wasn't too concerned. We understood the need for doctors to give the impression that they were able to do something for their patients, and we knew that zinc, in appropriate quantities, at least, caused no harm. Essentially, clinicians were leveraging a placebo effect, which has a non-medicinal therapeutic value, at the very least. However, the same cannot be said of ivermectin.

Developed in the 1970s, ivermectin is used to treat parasitic infections in livestock and as a low-cost, highly effective treatment for diseases in humans caused by parasites. In Nigeria, ivermectin is extensively used to treat onchocerciasis (river blindness). We were naturally excited about its potential value on SARS-CoV-2, given our familiarity with the medicine. However, before considering it for its potential value to the public, I needed to see data from clinical trials demonstrating improved outcomes among COVID-19 patients. As studies began to emerge, the data seemed flawed, and there was no consensus among the mainstream scientific community that it had any effect. On March 31, WHO advised that the current evidence on the use of ivermectin to treat COVID-19 patients was inconclusive and recommended that the drug only be used within clinical trials. I decided that NCDC would continue to focus on science and refrain from promoting unproven treatments, including ivermectin.

Growing up in an academic environment had a significant impact on my life. I was always fascinated by global advances driven by scientific discovery and realised that there were no shortcuts. I attribute this to the early lessons I learnt about the necessary thoroughness of the process of scientific discovery, especially with medical interventions.

Despite my insistence that neither chloroquine, Madagascar syrups, nor ivermectin had any effect, their use couldn't be stopped in our complex country where the channels for purchase and distribution are loose. Many doctors managing COVID patients in

Nigeria continued to prescribe ivermectin. When I challenged them, I would often be told: "It works for my patients."

There appeared to be a significant gap in the understanding of how viruses cause disease and that most viral diseases are self-limiting; some people will recover on their own even without treatment. For most infectious diseases, except for rabies, a proportion of those infected will survive regardless of intervention. For example, approximately 30% of those infected with Ebola virus or about 98% of those infected with COVID will survive. While those who survive may have received some therapeutics during their treatment, it is essential to note that not all substances administered are necessary for their recovery.

The it-works-for-my-patients concept may have a place in certain areas of medicine, but it has no place in the management of patients with infectious diseases. It is impossible to determine the cause of improvement in patient outcomes without clinical trials. To identify the effect of a particular intervention, appropriate control groups with similar characteristics, who didn't receive the treatment, must be included in the study. Clinical trials typically have four distinct phases, after which an identified drug can be approved by relevant bodies. Trials are essential in the development and implementation of effective treatments for diseases and involve a collaboration between academic experts, national public health institutes and regulatory bodies.

When I first started at NCDC, our main academic partners were the University of Ibadan and Ahmadu Bello University, Zaria. These institutions supported our field epidemiology training program, but I felt we could benefit from a more extensive collaboration. Unfortunately, our organisation lacked the resources to fully integrate them into our team, as we were unable to offer the same level of benefits they received at the universities. I stayed committed to finding ways to involve more academics in our work, with faith that their expertise would significantly strengthen our capacity to respond to public health challenges.

An NCDC collaboration with academia that I'm most proud of was our work on antimicrobial resistance (AMR). In 2017, at the World Health Assembly, AMR was a major topic on the agenda, and Member States were expected to present their situation analysis and progress in developing their National Action Plans. The Minister of Health, Professor Adewole assigned the task of developing Nigeria's Antimicrobial Resistance agenda to NCDC, with a specific mandate to be ready with our National Action Plan in less than six months.

This was a significant challenge for us at NCDC, but I was fortunate to have the support of a dear friend and colleague, Prof Iruka Okeke, who had just returned to Nigeria and had taken up an appointment to develop a new department at the University of Ibadan. I had immense respect for her work over the years; and through her, I met another colleague, Prof Oladipo Aboderin of the Obafemi Awolowo University, Ile-Ife, Osun State. Together with a team at NCDC, we collaborated to develop our National Action Plan for Antimicrobial Resistance. To the pleasant surprise of the Minister, we met the tight deadline. Prof Okeke and Prof Aboderin have continued to support NCDC's work and have become strong allies in the development of science in Nigeria. Their dedication and determination to develop scientists with an eye for service have inspired an entire generation of experts, who have worked with NCDC and beyond.

The African Centre for Genomics of Infectious Diseases (ACEGID), led by Professor Christian Happi at Redeemer's University, was also an early collaborator. Prof Happi's centre is a highly regarded institution in the field of genomics in Nigeria and Africa, and it was natural for us to partner with him as the pandemic evolved and variants emerged. They had previously helped us sequence samples from Lassa fever, yellow fever, and monkeypox outbreaks. His centre performed sequencing of samples across states, coordinated by NCDC. This partnership was instrumental in characterising the first sequence of SARS-CoV-2 from Africa, which led to a better understanding of the epidemiology of the disease as it spread.

A constraint in the building of our academic capacity was the overall education system in the country. In early 2022, university lecturers embarked on a prolonged strike action for nearly eight months—an entire academic year wasted. Strikes are a recurring issue insufficiently addressed by politicians. Unfortunately, strikes yield little progress, and the educational infrastructure continues to deteriorate in primary, secondary, and tertiary institutions. As a result, many lecturers and teachers are leaving the public sector in search of better opportunities in the private sector or abroad. As with the health sector, the government's annual allocation to education in the national budget is very low. It was especially unfortunate to witness, considering that Nigeria is home to many talented individuals who achieve exceptional success in various fields abroad.

The state of our education system also has a knock-on effect on the public health workforce. Deficits in the education system place a considerable burden on workplaces to provide training for new recruits. For instance, many laboratory scientists who were recruited to work at NCDC's reference laboratory and other public health laboratories across the country didn't have the opportunity to learn molecular methods while in university. Consequently, it was up to NCDC to provide training to these scientists after recruitment. Without this, they couldn't work in our laboratories.

As we began to collect data and track the spread of the outbreak, we found that mathematical models were required to make projections and plan for the future. Even though we could gather enough contextual and state surveillance data, we lacked the necessary resources to make accurate projections since there was no expertise to develop our own modelling capacity. We received offers for assistance from individuals and institutions outside of Nigeria, and there were many requests for access to Nigeria's data for mathematical modelling. But I didn't have the bandwidth to engage with them. At the same time, I knew that exchanging data without ensuring a commitment to developing Nigeria's capacity held no long-term benefits. I needed to find someone with the right expertise and a shared passion for Nigeria's development, which prompted me to consult a long-time colleague and friend, Prof Ibrahim Abubakar.

Ibrahim Abubakar was the Director of UCL's Global Health Programme and later became the Dean of the School of Population Sciences. He is a dedicated Nigerian whose advice I frequently relied on. Ibrahim had already demonstrated his commitment to improving Nigeria's health system as the chairperson of *The Lancet* Nigeria Commission[4], which brought together a diverse group of academics, scientists, epidemiologists, and other public health professionals to assess the state of the Nigerian health sector and make recommendations for the future. Recognising his expertise and passion, I asked for his support in managing the different offers of support on modelling. He advised that we form the 'Tuesday Evening Group,' which included colleagues from the National Bureau of Statistics, the National Institute for Medical Research (NIMR), the African Field Epidemiology Network, and the Federal Ministry of Health. Every week, they met and worked on generating modelling outputs, providing briefing papers for the PTF; these papers were crucial in responding to difficult policy questions such as decisions on lockdown, resumption of international travel, and others. Their

4 The LANCET Nigeria Report, written by a team of Nigeria experts working at institutions in country and around the world, developed recommendations to reposition future health policy to achieve universal health coverage and better health for all Nigerians. https://nigeriacommission.org/

contributions were invaluable, and they helped us make evidence-based decisions during a critical time.

Apart from Ibrahim's work, we established the Nigeria COVID-19 Research Consortium (NCRC) in collaboration with the Tertiary Education Trust Fund (TETFund), which brought together researchers and funders. The objective was to create a national platform for coordinating COVID-19 research and development activities, following WHO's global research roadmap. I co-chaired the consortium along with a trusted colleague, Prof Babatunde Salako, the Director General of NIMR. Dr Chinwe Ochu, NCDC's Director of Research, managed the secretariat. We collaborated with experts from various institutions to develop a research agenda for COVID-19; TETFund provided some initial funding to support the secretariat, and NCDC covered the remaining. The group successfully delivered several research outputs on COVID-19 from Nigeria, and I was proud of our collaborative, conflict-free approach. These two instances of collaboration between academia and the public health workforce are models I hope to see replicated and sustained in Nigeria. However, not all collaborations went as smoothly.

Several months into the response in Nigeria, in a surprising move, the Minister of Health established a committee of mostly senior academics to advise him on the pandemic response. While it was his prerogative on whom to consult, it would have been more beneficial to all if he had consulted me on the matter, but I respected his choice as the Minister. Surprisingly, the entire committee was invited to our Monday morning briefing, previously limited to the senior management of the Ministry of Health and planned to be a rapid one-hour session. The meetings became dominated by questions from the 'Ministerial Expert Advisory Committee on COVID-19,' causing them to last for hours. It wasn't the best use of my mornings, especially on Mondays. But I remained respectful, patiently answering all their questions even when I had reservations.

To my dismay, I started noticing that some of the strongest public criticism of Nigeria's response came from members of this committee; they would often utilise the privileged information gathered from the meetings in their pushback. Still, I held back—until an incident tipped me over the edge.

The Ministerial Expert Advisory Committee on COVID-19 applied to a department in WHO for funds to conduct a seroprevalence study in Nigeria without consulting NCDC. We were already conducting a similar study, which had been completed in four states[5]. It seemed like a waste of resources and an unnecessary duplication of our efforts. It was frustrating that this WHO department did not consult NCDC, before giving funds to an independent group in Nigeria. Furthermore, the results of their study were never published, which made me question the true intentions behind this study. It was disconcerting for me to observe how members of the committee were simultaneously advisers, insiders, chief critics, and implementers. It created a conflict of interest that I couldn't reconcile. It is important to have diverse perspectives and constructive criticism in any response, but it must be done with transparency and a clear understanding and demarcation of roles and responsibilities. Otherwise, it can lead to confusion, duplication of efforts, and ultimately, an ineffective response.

Improving public health is a goal shared by academia and public health agencies. While progress has been made in certain areas such as maternal health and fighting diseases like HIV, tuberculosis, and malaria, urgent attention must be given to epidemic preparedness and response. This can be challenging for academics who are more comfortable with hypothesis-driven research, but we must learn

5 The Seroprevalence SARS-CoV-2 in four states of Nigeria in October 2020: A population-based household survey was published by PLOS Global Public Health. https://journals.plos.org/globalpublichealth/article?id=10.1371/journal.pgph.0000363

from experience and work together to strengthen collaboration. By doing so, we can make a meaningful difference in the lives of people all around the world. The pandemic was a painful reminder of our vulnerability to new and emerging diseases. It also highlighted the importance of investing in research and development of treatments and vaccines in preparation for future outbreaks. I hope that Nigeria provides an even greater contribution to this.

ATTENUATION

"Nothing in life is to be feared, it is only to be understood. Now is the time to understand more, so that we may fear less."

Marie Curie

16

CLOSE TO HOME

By October 2020—the end of the first wave of the pandemic in Nigeria—there were over 68,000 confirmed cases with 1,173 deaths. By the end of November 2020, we began to record a spike in cases, in what is now infamously known as the 'second wave.'

Managing the public health response to the COVID-19 pandemic was undoubtedly the most difficult professional challenge I have faced in my career. The weight of providing credible leadership in a country with a population of approximately 200 million people was immense. I felt the burden of this responsibility every step of the way, every single day, as I strived to ensure that I didn't let the country down, with life throwing me a curveball of my own.

In January 2020, I went for my annual health check, thinking it would be just another routine visit. But my doctor noticed something that made him uncomfortable, and he ordered some more tests. By February, just before the index case in Nigeria and when preparedness plans were in full swing, the results came in. I had a serious medical condition that would require a significant surgical procedure. Vivianne and I were naturally concerned. As the leader of the agency responsible for the public health response to the pandemic, I knew I couldn't drop the responsibility of preparing my country for what was to come, yet my health was at stake. We weighed our options; however, the doctor recommended that it was ideal to have the surgery as soon as possible, but we could hold off for a bit, maybe a month or so.

We had to make a difficult decision: deal with this situation immediately or put my health concerns on hold to focus on leading the pandemic response. We soldiered on, hoping that the intensity of our response would soon bring the pandemic under control. Vivianne was always fully supportive, understanding the complexity of the situation we were in. In the intervening months, we didn't speak about it too often, but it lingered in the air. I will forever be grateful to my doctor, who kept reassuring us that a few months delay wouldn't make a significant difference. But as the pandemic raged, and the months dragged on, I wondered, what price would I pay for putting off the surgery for so long? Would I ever get *the* breather I needed to fix my health?

In August, I finally found a window to have the surgery. Cases were declining globally and in Nigeria—the end of what became known as the first wave. I was completely distracted by the demands of the pandemic, but I prepared myself as much as I could, both mentally and physically. I hoped that my absence wouldn't be too disruptive to the response effort, but I was confident that the team at NCDC was fully capable of leading the response, even in my absence. I handed over to Mrs Nwando Mba, the Director of Public Health Laboratory Services at NCDC, who was also the most senior Director at the time. She did an incredible job of managing all aspects of the response in my absence. Of course, being away was difficult, but I had regular phone calls with Mrs Mba, and I remained fully abreast of the response. Without her support, being away would have been much harder. I also had the support of Boss Mustapha, the PTF chair, who treated me like a brother and helped me through this tough time. While preparing for my surgery, I participated in virtual activities, including media interviews.

Figure 20: Walking into our regular COVID press briefing with Mr Boss Mustapha. Photo credit: Ifeoluwa Ojo/IKP Studios

In the lead-up to the surgery, I reflected on the last six months of 2020. I was constantly away from my family, juggling the demands of a global pandemic. I missed out on so much, and it made me feel very guilty. Now that things had slowed down a little bit, I had to explain to our boys that I had to undergo surgery, which was even harder than being away. Though uncertain of the recovery process, I was confident in my family's unwavering support, and it brought me peace.

From the PTF briefings—handled by Mrs Ilori, our Director of Surveillance—I learnt the media was speculating about the reasons for my absence. I was fortunate to have the strong support of my colleagues at NCDC, who respected my privacy and kept my medical situation confidential. Their professionalism, consideration, and unshaken diligence were invaluable during this sensitive time. With Vivianne by my side, we faced the uncertainty of the procedure and the long road to recovery. I'm most pleased to say that the surgery was a success, and I returned to work in September 2020. Indeed, all things worked together for good.

17

A SEAT ON THE GLOBAL STAGE

After my diagnosis in early 2020, I underwent a minor surgical intervention to determine the severity of my condition. I remember regaining consciousness as the anaesthesia wore off to find Vivianne by my bedside, seated on an armchair; she exuded a balmy aura that was welcoming and comforting. My mind spiralled in many directions, and I felt eerily light. I felt weak, like my insides were caving in on me, leaving me to my own devices. Groggily, I asked Vivianne how the procedure had gone, and she gently informed me that the surgeons assured her it had gone well. The tissue that had been removed by biopsy needed to be sent off for more testing. We chatted for a few minutes before I drifted back to sleep, not waking up till hours later. When I woke, even in this fragile moment, I jolted into action—or at least I tried to.

I remembered an important teleconference that I had agreed to join that evening, and asked Vivianne to please fetch my phone. The look on her face was a mix of terror, bewilderment, and worry. A look that suggested I was crazy to take a phone call right after surgery, but then again, she understood that we were in desperate times, and you know what they say about desperate times requiring equally desperate measures. It was difficult to explain the importance of the call, but as a unit, Vivianne and I had become accustomed to the unexpected. Vivianne was more than aware of the 'important' phone calls I often had to take and how rapidly situations could change. I felt much stronger and more rested, so I was ready for the scheduled phone call.

The call was convened by the Director General of WHO, Dr Tedros Adhanom Ghebreyesus, an informal platform for public health leaders around the world to discuss the ongoing pandemic. I recognised many voices on the call—colleagues that I had engaged with for years—who were also experts in their own field. There was no formal agenda, and no minutes were taken. Instead, the goal was to share insights and intelligence in a safe space, and to align our communication as much as possible. The tension in people's voices was palpable when the anticipated explosion of cases in Africa was discussed, considering the already weak health systems in the region. Meanwhile, there was a sense of assurance among leaders in more developed countries, who generally believed they could weather the storm. Despite the uncertainties and challenges, the call provided an opportunity for leaders to speak openly, think together, and support each other during an unprecedented global crisis.

During this crucial call, a colleague I had worked with and come to admire used the phrase 'Facts Not Fear,' which stuck with me throughout the pandemic. This phrase stuck with me throughout the pandemic. It was a simple yet powerful reminder that we needed to stay focused on the facts and evidence, rather than yield to fearmongering or speculation. I was struck by the clarity and wisdom of those three words, and they would continue to guide me in the months and years ahead. All through the first wave, our informal group continued to convene whenever Dr Tedros needed a safe space to discuss critical issues. Sometimes, the meetings were chaired by Dr Mike Ryan when the demands on the DG's time increased.

In addition to the WHO DG's informal group, members of NCDC team, including myself, were invited to participate in a wide range of committees convened by WHO, Africa CDC and several other regional and global bodies. These new groups were tasked with making difficult decisions that would have overarching consequences for public health and the global economy. It was a humbling experience working alongside experts from around the world, witnessing the level of dedication and expertise that went into shaping a global response.

On a quiet Sunday, while trying to catch a desperately needed nap, my phone rang. By now, it must be obvious that my phone never rung for a meagre reason. This time, it was my dear friend and brother from the Africa-CDC, John Nkengasong. We exchanged warm greetings before he informed me that he was considering NCDC for the leadership of a small group to develop and support the implementation of Infection Prevention and Control measures against the virus.

Figure 21: One of my regular meetings with John Nkengasong, Director of Africa Centres for Disease Control. Photo credit: Ifeoluwa Ojo/IKP Studios

I was anxious about how we could handle this added responsibility alongside other tasks, but declining wasn't an option. We had to support our brothers and sisters in the region. After the call, I asked my colleague Dr Tochi Okwor to lead this engagement on our behalf. Tochi had been at the forefront of creating a new Infection Prevention and Control unit at NCDC, so she embraced this challenge with enthusiasm and vigour. Working alongside colleagues in the Africa CDC, with other countries and partners, they developed robust guidance to support countries in the fight against the pandemic. Tochi did an outstanding job and has grown exponentially ever since, participating in numerous global infection prevention and control efforts.

Africa CDC's ability to lead the continent in several technical areas where they lacked internal capacity was a subject of much discussion and speculation. The not-so-well-kept secret behind their success was the careful and intentional recruitment of colleagues from across the continent. For instance, Amadou Sall, Director of Institut Pasteur in Dakar was brought in to support the development of strategies for diagnostics, while Alan Christoffels, Christian Happi, and Tulio de Oliveira were recruited to support genomic surveillance. This mutually beneficial arrangement allowed experts to work together towards a common goal and provided opportunities for professional growth and development.

Besides leading Nigeria's response to the pandemic, I strongly believed in the importance of participating in global discussions and collaboration. I was frequently invited to comment on current global issues, wherein I presented fresh perspective from Africa. I found different channels to express my views, including through editorials and social media. For me, it wasn't just about leading an organisation, but developing a stronger voice in global affairs, especially when it came to the progress of our continent. I always felt personally embarrassed when relevant African voices made little contribution to conversations that affected us on the continent.

I must say that I consider many global leaders my close friends—and have no doubt about their competence and good intentions—but I'm often uncertain about how well they appreciate the depth and complexity of the challenges on our continent. I believe having more colleagues from Africa playing greater leadership roles in global health organisations would be incredibly beneficial to everyone. These roles require not only technical competence, but also empathy and compassion, which I believe can only be developed with time and experience. Global health indices will benefit greatly from more diverse representation at all levels of leadership. Given that I was often one of the few African voices in the room, I had to be intentional about when and how I used it. There were small victories, but most of these opinions went unheeded and the world continued to operate as usual, with wealthy countries purchasing and hoarding far more vaccines than they needed. Nonetheless, I remained cognisant that we needed to continue building and advocating for more local interest and resources on the issues that were important to us in our own countries.

I believe we could have taken more lessons on pandemic response from middle-income countries facing similar demographic problems, like Brazil, India, Indonesia, Egypt, and South Africa. These countries also have large populations and are experiencing both economic growth and challenging social conditions. Countries in Africa seem to be undergoing parallel development, when we could benefit more from a symbiotic association. It is important to foster exchange and collaboration between countries to facilitate sharing of knowledge, resources, and best practices. Together, we can overcome the public health challenges on our continent.

18

TANGENTS OF TURBULENCE

In early October, another looming crisis imploded.

Young people across the country took to the streets, calling for the disbandment of the Special Anti-Robbery Squad (SARS), a notorious unit of the Nigerian Police Force known for its history of brutality and corruption. The protests gained momentum and evolved into the #EndSARS movement. I had never seen this magnitude of resistance, especially among the youth. Even though I had concerns, I was inspired by young people coming together and finding their voices, vehemently demanding for change. The protests weren't merely about police brutality, but also about the wider economic challenges and the impact of the ongoing pandemic. The fact that this 'specialist' police force was targeting young people who were struggling to make a living only served to further ignite their anger and determination to fight for justice.

On October 20, after weeks of peaceful protests, security forces responded with brutal force in the Lekki area of Lagos, where the protestors had peacefully gathered. As more people poured onto the streets, I grew increasingly concerned because this coincided with a surge in COVID-19 cases. With vaccines only recently approved globally, we were still uncertain about when Nigeria would receive its first shipment. Also, I hadn't anticipated the direct threat to NCDC staff and property. A breakdown in law and order followed leading to more riots and destruction of government-owned property across the country.

It was a time of great anxiety in the country, and our leaders appeared to be caught off-guard. This terrible situation was further exacerbated by the discovery of warehouses stacked with food items—or 'palliatives' as they were widely known—procured through CACOVID donations to alleviate the pandemic's impact. Many Nigerians, already struggling to feed themselves and their families due to the pandemic's impact on their livelihood, felt that their leaders didn't care about their well-being. The public believed these palliatives were hoarded by some state governments instead of being distributed to those in need. Nigerians felt betrayed and ignored. This frustration and anger resulted in more violent protests and rioting, with warehouses, treatment centres, laboratories, and hospital wards becoming targets of destruction.

One night, I received a distress call that rioters were attempting to break into the NCDC warehouse where we stored crucial medical supplies such as personal protective equipment and laboratory commodities. We tried to explain that the warehouse contained no food items or anything for domestic consumption, but the rioters continued to bang on the doors. I had a horrifying feeling that everything we had worked so hard to build would be destroyed in an instant. I reached out to the Minister of Health, who was uncertain about the best action to take and promised to get back to me. I didn't receive any follow-up from him. I remembered my colleague at the Office of the National Security Adviser (ONSA), Dr Levin Damisah, who had been working with us even before the pandemic. I immediately reached out to him for help, and he sent an elite military team to protect the warehouse, which they did by holding off the rioters until daybreak. The military team demonstrated remarkable restraint and attempted to reason with the protesters. Thanks to their efforts, we could preserve the essential medical supplies and equipment we worked tirelessly to procure, much of it through donations from multilateral partners. Without their intervention, the consequences could have been catastrophic, unleashing untold damage to public health in Nigeria.

The situation de-escalated after hours of negotiation with the protestors. I went out to meet them personally with a few select members of my team and tried to explain that we were on the same side. Eventually, they agreed to select three leaders who would be taken into the warehouse to examine its contents and confirm that there were no food items or 'palliatives' stored inside. This calmed things down and some of the rioters dissipated, but a few hundred remained insistent on getting in. To ensure the safety of our commodities, the military team stayed in place for three days before stating that they had to attend to other duties. They provided NCDC with a warehouse within their compound, which was more secure. In October 2020, just before the second wave of COVID-19, we had to move all our commodities to a military warehouse. Throughout this episode, two young members of NCDC team stayed involved from the beginning to the end, negotiating, and ensuring the safety of our commodities—Elder Muhammed and Darlington Ugwu. I am sure they learnt a lot from this episode, despite the challenges at the time.

With the second wave now in full swing, we not only had to contend with containing the spread of the virus but also ensure the safety of critical medical supplies and equipment. The threat of violence and unrest blurred the line between maintaining public health and public safety. It was a daunting task, and I often wondered if the leaders of other national public health agencies were facing similar obstacles. We had to take drastic measures to protect the safety of NCDC staff; misinformation and conspiracy theories about the pandemic were spreading and some members of the public started to harass our team, making it unsafe to be seen as an NCDC staff. We had to remove any identifying markers from our vehicles and implement vehicle tracking devices to ensure the safety of our teams. We also raised staff awareness on how to stay secure in various environments. But our efforts weren't enough to save one of our own.

On October 4, a deeply personal and painful tragedy occurred. Around the same time as the #EndSARS protests, armed men attacked an NCDC vehicle and fatally shot Uche Njoku, a dedicated member of our team. Uche, along with Pius, an NCDC driver, had travelled to one of the states to deliver emergency supplies, which was a routine task for us. This sad incident transpired when states were struggling to keep up with the demand for tests and we were racing against time to replenish their supplies. Despite our strict guidelines for interstate travel, Uche and Pius decided to undertake the journey late into the night after being stuck in traffic earlier in the day. As they made their way back, they were ambushed by armed men who opened fire on their vehicle. Uche was struck by a bullet and died instantly. He had only recently joined NCDC as a volunteer, and his hard work and commitment led to him becoming a contractor during the pandemic. He was always devoted to service, and his death was a devastating loss.

We did everything we could to support our team after the tragic loss. We knew we had to keep going, even though it felt impossible a lot of times. Uche's death was a painful reminder of the risks we faced every day, especially as the security situation in Nigeria continued to deteriorate. I vividly remember visiting Uche's family at their home on the outskirts of Owerri. His parents were grief-stricken and lost for words—inconsolable even. I barely had the right words to say, but what can one possibly say to sooth the pain of a child's death? We could only be there for them, offering our support in any way we could. Uche's death increased our worries about the safety of our team. We often had to make tough calls to establish regions that were safe enough to deploy our teams to, especially when there was a public health threat.

The following year, we lost one of our brightest, young pharmacists, Love Omoniyei. I first met Love in 2018 while he was working for one of our partner organisations, and I was impressed by his humility, intelligence, and infectious positivity. He was quite popular among staff. When we had the opportunity to hire new recruits, Love applied and was offered a position at NCDC. He was very excited to join us, and we were eager to have him contribute to the expansion of our existing AMR functions. Sometime later, on a normal working day, colleagues noticed that Love hadn't reported to the office for a few days, which was very unusual. Love was found dead in his apartment. We let the authorities do their job, but there were no signs of wrongdoing. It was a sudden and devastating loss for us all, and it was particularly hard to cope with, as it came just a year after Uche's death.

As we grieved the loss of another member of the NCDC team, we made sure to provide support and counselling for our staff, especially the young ones who were close to Love. We also visited Love's family to offer our condolences and assure them of our support. These visits were some of the most difficult days for me and my colleagues at NCDC. Losing a member of staff, especially one so young and full of promise, was a continued reminder of how fragile life can be. We had to be extremely sensitive to the mental health of our team, and we worked hard to create a supportive environment for everyone during this difficult time. I'm incredibly proud of the resilience and tenacity shown by the NCDC team. They remained steadfast in their mission to protect the health of Nigerians, even in the face of immense pressure, attacks, and deaths.

As the leader of NCDC, it wasn't always easy to stay focused and motivated. Fortunately, I had the unwavering support of Vivianne, who not only helped keep my spirits up, but also cooperated with the NCDC team and our crisis communication partners. She was always up to date on my daily challenges and stresses, which made a significant difference. Additionally, Vivianne had the added responsibility of ensuring that our sons were coping with the changes brought on by the pandemic, including attending classes online. My daily schedule restricted me from giving them my undivided attention, but Vivianne assiduously filled this gap, keeping our family together during turbulent times.

19

LEVERAGING HERD IMMUNITY

During the acute phase of the pandemic, COVAX was created to enable the equitable access to COVID-19 vaccines. COVAX was co-led by WHO, GAVI, CEPI, and UNICEF to ensure that countries all over the world, especially low-income countries, had access to the vaccines; however, many countries were left waiting for their doses, while watching rich countries vaccinate their citizens and stockpile millions of doses. I had a feeling the inequitable access to COVID-19 diagnostics during the first year of the pandemic would play out in the second year on a much larger scale with vaccines, and countries in Africa—including Nigeria—would bear the brunt of this inequity. It was heart-breaking hearing stories of health care workers in several countries, who were on the frontlines of the pandemic without proper protection, let alone a vaccine. This was the reality of the world we lived in.

In February 2021, almost a year after my first visit to Wuhan, I received an invitation to write a commentary for the China CDC Weekly—a scientific journal published by the country's centre for disease control. My stance was clear: the situation in Africa was appalling. Nigeria had recorded its first case a year ago, yet only three African countries (Guinea, Egypt, and the Seychelles) had started the administration of vaccines. Meanwhile, more than 100 million vaccine doses had been administered in about 60 other countries outside of the region. It sure felt like the rest of the world accepted this as the norm, solely focusing on securing doses for themselves. It seemed as though high-income countries had gone into self-preservation mode, and I couldn't shake my disappointment and frustration. This wasn't the way the world should have responded to a global pandemic, especially not after pushing the narrative of togetherness. Yet, it felt like there wasn't much I, or anyone else in our region, could do about the situation. So much for global solidarity!

Figure 22: Finally the vaccines arrive in Nigeria
Photo credit: Ifeoluwa Ojo/IKP Studios

NCDC played a leading role in the public health response to the pandemic in Nigeria, but our primary mandate didn't include access to vaccines or immunisation efforts. Instead, this fell under the purview of our sister agency, the National Primary Health Care Development Agency (NPHCDA), led by Dr Faisal Shuaib, a colleague who I worked with throughout the response. I deferred to his leadership on this issue and refrained from publicly engaging the slow global distribution of vaccines. New variants of the virus were emerging, and population immunity was the only chance we had against the virus; if we weren't all immunised, we risked a drastic relapse.

As NPHCDA led our vaccine efforts, NCDC shifted its focus to following the global vaccine discourse, including issues of vaccine research, development, and distribution, as well as decisions on prioritising special populations to receive the scarce vaccines. In my commentary for China CDC, I described COVAX as 'an extraordinary and unique global collaboration with the aim of providing innovative and equitable access to COVID-19 vaccines.' I firmly believed in the intentions of its founding institutions and in multilateralism in the fight against the pandemic, but I was deeply disappointed by the delays in delivery.

With time, the focus of the PTF press briefings shifted from updates about the COVID-19 cases in the country to questions about when Nigeria would access vaccines. We were constantly bombarded with queries about timelines for accessing vaccines, and it was difficult to respond because we didn't know when we would receive any supplies. Weeks turned into months, and it became apparent that the reliance on a global solidarity mechanism was insufficient in a world with unequal access to resources and power. After what seemed like a few 'false starts,' we finally received a shipment of nearly four million doses of Oxford-AstraZeneca vaccine on March 21, 2021. This was a seminal moment, the start of a new chapter in our fight against the pandemic.

A large team of leaders across the health sector, including myself, went to the airport to receive the vaccines, and we took timestamped pictures to document the occasion. It felt like we had been waiting for this day for so long, and finally, we had more tools to fight back against the virus. NPHCDA developed deployment strategies, prioritising vulnerable populations. As members of the PTF, we were invited to publicly receive our doses to build trust and address vaccine hesitancy among the public. With cameras rolling and the entire nation watching, I took a deep breath and braced myself for the prick. I let out a small gasp as the needle pierced through my skin, not because it was painful, but because it was such a historic moment. This marked the beginning of our public vaccination exercise.

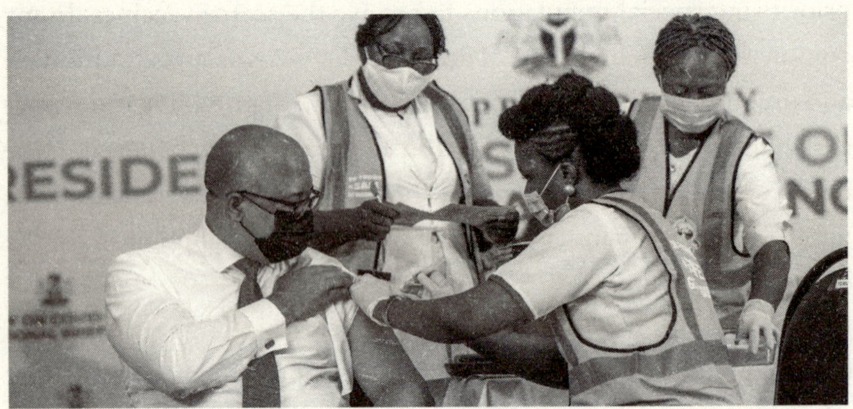

Figure 23: Receiving the COVID vaccine on national television.
Photo credit: Ifeoluwa Ojo/IKP Studios

We took the vaccine to the Presidential Villa, where the President and Vice President received their doses on camera. It was reassuring for Nigerians to see their leaders leading by example, while their personal physicians oversaw the administration of the vaccine. The arrival of the vaccines was a huge relief for us all, but we knew that convincing the public to take them would be a strenuous battle. We faced hesitancy from the outset. Many people were sceptical about the vaccine, and it would take time and effort to educate the public about its safety and efficacy. The distrust was rife; a friend told me that they didn't trust the vaccine and would rather rely on traditional remedies. It was a frustrating, but unsurprising comment—Nigerians have always had a deep-seated distrust of its public sector. Besides, vaccine resistance was a global problem. Now that we had vaccines, we had to build trust and combat misinformation to achieve decent administration rates.

Before the vaccine rollout began, the Ministry of Communications made a perplexing announcement, requiring all Nigerians to register for a National Identification Number (NIN) by a certain date or risk losing access to their mobile numbers. The registration involved biometric capturing, which caused long queues and overcrowding at registration centres across the country. This announcement was made during the holiday season, and at a time when we were concerned about a surge in cases. Unfortunately, it also provided a perfect opportunity for the spread of misinformation about the pandemic and vaccines. I remember reading ridiculous stories on social media about the government creating opportunities for COVID-19 to spread, so that more funds could be allocated to the purchase of vaccines. This was particularly absurd given that the Nigerian government hadn't purchased any vaccines at the time. It was disheartening to see how easily people fell for these stories and how it further fuelled vaccine hesitancy in the country.

While hesitancy among the public wasn't surprising, I wasn't prepared for hesitancy among health workers, and it was truly difficult to wrap my mind around it. If the very people who had seen the devastation of COVID-19 up close were unsure about the safety and effectiveness of the vaccines, how could we convince the rest of the population? To make matters worse, stories of supposed harmful effects of the vaccines began to spread like wildfire on WhatsApp, Nigeria's most popular messaging app and a consistent source of rumours and misinformation. Every day unearthed a new conspiracy theory about the vaccines, even among those who should have known better. I believe this experience taught us a lot about our country and the work required to curb such unfounded pushback. Science communication and informing the public about vaccine development would have prepared the public in the months before the vaccine arrival.

I think the lack of trust between the government and its citizens was the biggest source of vaccine hesitancy. This distrust extended to healthcare workers, who were actively protesting against the non-payment of hazard allowances. In one meeting with healthcare workers where the vaccine rollout plan was discussed, distrust was a recurrent issue. One of the nurses said that she didn't believe the government cared about their well-being, so why should they trust the government's vaccine? It was a difficult question to answer, but we surmised that we had our work cut out for us to rebuild that trust. We needed to show that we were committed to the health and well-being of our citizens and healthcare workers. We started by providing more transparent information about the vaccine, addressing rumours and misinformation as they arose. Slowly but surely, we began to see a shift in attitudes towards the vaccine.

Figure 24: On a visit to our colleagues in a special vaccination booth. Photo credit: Ifeoluwa Ojo/IKP Studios

NCDC used the opportunity to re-evaluate our priorities on the response, making sure that investments served a long-term purpose. We mounted a vigorous campaign to support states and teaching hospitals across Nigeria with new infectious disease laboratories and treatment centres. Resources were allocated to tertiary hospitals around the country, advocating and supporting each of them to have at least a molecular laboratory and a purpose-built infectious disease ward. In some of these, we also supported the establishment of warehouses to store resources needed to manage infectious disease cases.

We were creative in our approach of supporting NPHCDA with ensuring vaccine compliance, engaging with community leaders, religious leaders, and other influencers to help spread the message about the safety and efficacy of the vaccines. We continued to build our healthcare infrastructure, including expanding our laboratory network and improving our disease surveillance systems. As the second wave of the pandemic waned, we reflected on what we had learnt and achieved, and categorised the work left, refusing rest until all Nigerians had access to the vaccines needed to protect themselves and their loved ones. It was our hope that in the coming months and years, we would continue to make progress towards achieving this goal—for COVID-19 and beyond.

20

NOTES ON LEADERSHIP

During my time in office, I was privileged to acquire first-hand understanding of the unique challenges facing the country's public sector institutions. These institutions heavily rely on their leaders to define their fate, which unavoidably results in vulnerability; if the leader fails, the entire organisation fails. With the benefit of hindsight and a tinge of nostalgia, I can look back at my time as DG of NCDC and delineate what I learnt on the job.

My first undertaking on resumption was to connect with my new colleagues. I wanted to understand their motivation and assess their understanding of their responsibilities. What I found was surprising, confusing, and concerning. Most did not seem to have a coherent reply, including very senior colleagues. As I probed further, it became clear that no one had ever asked them these questions, and they were simply going through the motions. One senior colleague showed me copies of a strategic plan that had been drafted a few years ago by an external consultant. They admitted that none of them had been part of its development and most weren't aware of its existence. There was a huge disconnect between the leadership and the staff, and a need to bridge that gap to create a more effective organisation.

Nearly everyone had a general idea of what they were doing, but there was no unified mission to guide the work. Serious work was needed to clarify our purpose. Without a strategic direction, or defined roles, our early efforts appeared disjointed and uncoordinated. What surprised me even more was that no one had a job description. Rather than charge into action, I had to hold back on my big ideas and focus on fixing the many foundational issues. Before defining a vision and mobilising colleagues, I needed to understand the competencies of the people with whom I would be undertaking this journey and their perception of the agency's mission.

Following the initial meetings, I decided to set up more structured meetings with the team—individual and group meetings to gather feedback and identify challenges. I asked hard questions and pushed my colleagues to provide honest and constructive feedback. *"Forget that I'm DG,"* I urged. Many of them were doubtful; they were just not used to being asked for their opinions. Even when I assured them that their views wouldn't be used to form impressions of them and it was all for my own enlightenment, it was hard to get them to speak.

Slowly, with much prodding, people started to open up and share their stories, anxieties, hopes, and aspirations. Some of what I heard was depressing, but many were uplifting. *There is something here that I can work with*, I thought. I also used those meetings to share my new vision for the organisation, as well as my optimism about our future. It was inspiring to see how this singular move spurred eagerness about the prospect of working in a dynamic institution with societal relevance. Some even expressed gratitude for being consulted by the CEO and given the chance to contribute to the agency's direction, and I was deeply grateful to them for trusting me. The conversations always ended with me making a personal commitment to work hard for them, both individually and collectively. It was a powerful moment for me, knowing that my colleagues were willing to give me a chance as their leader, and I was determined to live up to their expectations. From these sessions, I decided that involving the team in the decision-making process and making them feel heard was crucial to building a strong and motivated team.

I reached out to anyone who could help, including former colleagues, friends, and even people I had met at events and conferences, who had specific areas of expertise. Many of the initial responses I got weren't positive. People shared stories about how they had been scarred in the past while trying to support public institutions in Nigeria and were worried about reputational risk. But I was determined and unassuaged. I reached out to Gbolahan Faleye, a staff member of the Tony Blair Institute (TBI) for Global Change, whom I met through my good friend Ike Anya. With a bit of persuasion, he agreed to provide some pro-bono support. He offered to bring in one of their most senior advisers, Nnaemeka Okafor who had just completed a project for Nigeria's previous Minister of Finance, Dr Ngozi Okonjo-Iweala. I knew that Emeka was used to working on high-profile projects, and I was worried that he wouldn't find NCDC as exciting as his previous work, but I was desperate and willing to take any help I could get. In addition to Gbolahan, I also reached out to a sister, friend, and colleague, Dr Ebere Okereke, who was working at the UK Health Security Agency (then Public Health England). Ebere didn't need much convincing and even took two weeks of annual leave to come and support me in my early weeks at NCDC. I was grateful beyond words but didn't know how to pay her for her time. To my surprise, she waived any payment and only asked for us to support her logistics.

With Ebere and Nnaemeka on board, I now started to feel like I had a team that could take on the challenges ahead. But we needed more support. I reached out to Patrick Nguku, who led the Africa Field Epidemiology Network (AFENET) in Nigeria. We had already started discussing how we could work together, and he agreed to pay for Ebere's transportation to Nigeria. And just like that, our first strategic team had been formed. The process of defining NCDC's goals, objectives, and activities wasn't easy, but we tackled it with enthusiasm and dedication. Emeka and Ebere were relentless in engaging with staff and reporting back to me. We spent hours debating, brainstorming, and discussing the best path forward. There were times we reached dead ends and had to recalibrate. But every time we did, we grew stronger and more focused on our mission.

Figure 25: A moment during a difficult phone call captured by NCDC
Photo credit: Ifeoluwa Ojo/IKP Studios

We convened a two-day brainstorming session with all staff in the Abuja office and invited some colleagues from the Lagos office. It was an opportunity for everyone to share their thoughts and ideas on how to move the agency forward. There were moments that felt so still and quiet, you could almost hear a pin drop—then someone would break the silence with a brilliant suggestion that sparked a lively discussion.

It was amazing to see the growing excitement of the staff to make NCDC a success. After weeks of hard work and collaboration, we had a solid plan that we were all proud of. Nnaemeka brought in a few other colleagues to work with us on developing our strategic plan, including Ope Adejoro who would work with us for many years to come. This was a game-changer for NCDC. All the late nights and hard work were worth it; we were certain.

The strategy plan was more than just a document. It was a compass that helped us navigate the choppy waters of a new organisation with a lofty mission. We printed copies for all our staff and presented some copies to our partners. It was always within arm's reach, and we often referred to it. From this point onwards, we convened regular progress meetings every three months and held each other accountable for the delivery of the goals we set for ourselves.

The initial sign of progress—given the daunting challenge—was humbling. It felt like we had released some inert energy in many people. At a meeting shortly after our plan was devised, a colleague we had sent to set up a laboratory system in one of the states beamed with pride as he showed us pictures of the newly installed equipment. He was given an award by the state government, and he was so excited. It was a small victory, yet I knew something transformational was happening to the team. Something that I had felt in my early days of working in Europe. The feeling of making a difference—of being seen. Of course, there were setbacks. There were times we realised that we needed to modify a certain objective, or that we had underestimated the resources needed to achieve it. But we never lost sight of our goal, which was to build a trusted institution that could protect Nigerians from deadly disease outbreaks. While we didn't meet every goal that we set out to achieve, I was confident that the ones we missed had clear reasons for not being met, and that our team had given their all regardless. When I left NCDC in 2021, I was indubitably proud of everything we achieved as a team.

21

THE PEOPLE BEHIND THE SCENES

At the beginning of my tenure, there were three major problems with the workforce at NCDC:

1. With less than 100 people in an agency serving 200 million people, we were severely understaffed.
2. The competency level amongst the existing personnel was generally inadequate for the standards NCDC was expected to deliver, though this wasn't the personnel's fault.
3. Despite their best intentions, most of the staff lacked the motivation required to put in the kind of effort that could transform the agency. The remuneration levels in the Nigerian public service simply couldn't incentivise people to put in that kind of effort.

To turn things around, we had to find ways of attracting talent, while motivating the existing staff to align with our vision for a stronger national public health agency. I spent a significant portion of the first few weeks searching for competent laboratory scientists, virologists, and epidemiologists to fill gaps in our workforce. Shortly into the process, I encountered significant obstacles due to bureaucratic red tape and limited resources. I tried the most obvious paths and was told they weren't possible, so I had to get creative with my recruitment efforts. This meant attracting staff to NCDC on secondment, focusing on those who were already in the public sector.

I reached out to two former colleagues who had also trained with me in the UK—Emmanuel Agogo and Priscilla Ibekwe. They had moved back to Nigeria a few years earlier and found employment at the National Agency for the Control of AIDS (NACA). Given our common history, I convinced them to join me. I also approached an old friend, Chibuzo Eneh, a pharmacist working with the National Agency for Food and Drug Administration and Control (NAFDAC). Although initially sceptical, I wore her down with my persuasion, and she eventually agreed. These three joined us as secondees from their agencies after I convinced their chief executive officers to support the development of our relatively small and young agency. I successfully persuaded my former colleague from the UK, Dr Olusola Aruna, to join our team in its initial stages, actively seeking partners' support to cover her allowances.

For many years, I had been aware of the Nigeria Field Epidemiology and Laboratory Training Programme, given that I had benefited from a similar programme in Europe. I reached out to Patrick Nguku who led the programme to send some senior fellows that hadn't yet returned to their primary positions. This would only last a few months and was a win-win situation—an avenue for exchanging knowledge and expertise. He agreed, sending three staff to join NCDC. They were: Chioma Dan-Nwafor, William Nwachukwu, and Biodun Ogunniyi.

These efforts enabled NCDC to assemble a talented group of colleagues to join our team. While their arrival sparked some excitement, not everyone was happy. Some felt threatened and said it was unfair to include outsiders in the emerging era when they hadn't been part of NCDC's foundation. I understood their concerns, but we had to build quickly and properly to tackle the urgent public health challenges facing the country. I couldn't commit to paying competitive salaries, but I believed we could support the development of our workforce if we delivered significant results in the short term. To achieve this, I had to lead by example. I worked long hours every day and showed the team that I was ready to contribute to every aspect of the agency's operations while empowering as many colleagues as possible to lead different initiatives. I prioritised their concerns and responded to every email promptly, often within 24 hours. I spent hours in meetings with staff and partners, listening to their issues and providing timely feedback.

In the Nigerian civil service, physical folders are the order of the day. They contain documents and records of various official transactions, such as memos, letters, reports, proposals, and approvals. These folders are used to manage official processes and are usually passed from one desk to another until they reach the final decision-maker. As part of my daily routine, I reviewed pending folders. My goal was to have cleared my desk by the end of each working day. To enhance our internal processes, I encouraged my team to establish a simple system to track the movement of files. These changes helped improve our turnaround time, prevent the loss of files, and minimise actionable backlogs. Colleagues were often surprised when they got a same-day response to a request that would usually take weeks to resolve.

I encouraged and challenged the staff to put in their best efforts towards achieving our goals, assuring them that the rewards will come. I wanted to create an environment where everyone felt valued, heard, and recognised for their contributions. Slowly, NCDC employees began to exhibit exceptional service, discipline, and sacrifice. They were more willing to go the extra mile to achieve our objectives, and their commitment to the agency's goals became more evident with each passing day. Our 'can do' attitude shone through. The staff felt more confident in their abilities and were encouraged to speak up, knowing that their voices would be heard. I was proud to witness this transformation. There were times I had to shut the door and dab a few tears, after all, leaders do not cry in Nigeria, right? I didn't want my tears to be mistaken for weakness.

We adopted the mantra, '*keep pushing*,' which I frequently used to rally staff members. I'm not quite sure how I arrived at this phrase but it seemed to resonate with people, so I started to sign off my emails and speeches with it. As a result of this newfound attitude, NCDC became an attractive agency to work for, and within a year, I received a flood of requests, especially from field epidemiology graduates who wanted to join our agency. They were all seeking an institution where they could serve their country. It was no longer business as usual in the public service. This was the beginning of the NCDC way.

Kola Jinadu, a young and talented intern, was 'working' at NCDC when I arrived in 2016. He had recently completed his residency in Public Health at the University of Ibadan, and I learnt he sought an opportunity to gain experience by volunteering with NCDC. He was working without pay, which wasn't sustainable and made me uncomfortable—but he had good skills, and I wanted to keep him. As I searched for funding options to officially onboard him, Kola received an offer to work with an international NGO. Although I was upset, we were losing such a talented young colleague, I was also happy for him.

Later, the opportunity to expand our team arose, following the passage of NCDC Act in 2018. Kola wasted no time in resigning from his NGO role and reapplying to join the agency. He expressed his deep desire to work towards our vision and contribute his skills to the organisation. It was heart-warming to see that we were still considered an attractive place to work, even to colleagues that had other options, and we were thrilled to welcome him back to the team. Kola's story wasn't unusual as NCDC became a much sought after place to work.

Finding innovative ways to support the growth and development of our young workforce despite not being able to afford competitive salaries was tricky. One thing I did was scout for training and mentorship opportunities, like those that I had benefited from earlier in my own career. Whenever our partners offered us training opportunities for one person, I would request at least three slots, arguing that Nigeria's size and population warranted more opportunities for equity. My persistence often paid off, so I proactively approached our partners, requesting training opportunities for our staff. Early into my tenure, we were offered just one slot at the US CDC training on public health emergency management. Our organisation was in dire need of this, so I reached out to the CDC and explained our situation. They were impressed by our determination and offered us an additional slot. Seeing the excitement and enthusiasm of our staff upon their return and hearing about their newfound knowledge made all the effort worthwhile.

I also actively sought opportunities for degree-granting programmes, knowing that advanced education would benefit NCDC as well as individual staff members. I spent hours editing resumes and motivation statements and writing detailed recommendation letters. More than 15 staff members secured fully funded scholarships for their master's or PhD programmes, and I was confident that many of them would be of service to NCDC in the short and long term.

My focus wasn't solely on colleagues in technical roles. I was also conscious of the support staff who played crucial roles in NCDC's operations. They are the unsung heroes of organisations, often overlooked and undervalued. For instance, our drivers play a vital role in safely transporting medical commodities to labs across the country. Without their dedication and hard work, we wouldn't have been able to respond effectively to health emergencies. We provided them with professional training and regular medical exams, just as we did for our technical colleagues. By recognising and valuing their contributions, we created a culture of respect and appreciation, which ultimately led to a more cohesive and effective team, led by the amiable Mr Shehu.

As I strolled through the NCDC office daily, I felt an overwhelming sense of pride and joy at the progress my colleagues had made. Many of them started as interns or entry-level staff, but had grown to taking on more responsibilities and managing projects on their own. Working with such a diverse team and seeing the impact of our collective effort was fulfilling. I always tried to connect with each person on a personal level and got to know them individually. Sometimes, I sat with a few of them to chat about their experiences at NCDC. They shared how they had grown in their roles and the support they received from colleagues and supervisors. Without a doubt, I could sense they felt valued and appreciated, and that NCDC had become more than just a job to them.

I found a strong ally in our Director of Administration, Mr Yakubu Abdullahi, who shared my passion for staff and organisational development. He would often show up in the office on Saturdays to ensure there were no unexpected challenges and that our operations ran smoothly in the coming week. On those Saturdays, he and I would walk around our buildings, inspecting the infrastructure. It was an incredible feeling seeing my colleagues thrive and grow. It wasn't just about the work we did, but also about the people we worked with and how we supported each other. Investing in the growth and development of our staff not only helped fill the skills gap, but also boosted confidence and motivation. Newfound skills translated into improved service delivery and increased morale, making NCDC a more attractive agency for young talent in Nigeria.

22

BUREAUCRATIC BATTLES

There had always been a strange resistance to NCDC's existence from some quarters within the Ministry of Health. It appeared that some staff felt the establishment of this new parastatal was taking away something crucial from them. In the beginning, I thought this was linked to the first national coordinator of the NCDC project (as it was earlier called), a retired director from the Ministry. Later, I realised that the issue was much deeper and began almost immediately the idea for the agency was conceived in 2011.

When the first memo proposing this new agency was signed by the permanent secretary at the time, staff in a few units of the Ministry were directed to move to the nascent NCDC. The leadership of the Ministry didn't adequately elaborate the need for this new agency, so this small, uncurbed rebellion persisted for many years and manifested itself in different ways, sometimes overtly, other times clandestine. The situation caused anxiety and uncertainty among staff who transferred to NCDC, and this active antagonism hindered the agency's progress in its early years—until the outbreak of Lassa fever in January 2016 rejuvenated this fragile team. The fledgling NCDC staff came together and worked hard to control the outbreak, distinguishing themselves and gaining the attention of the new Minister of Health, Professor Isaac Adewole, who was appointed towards the end of 2016. This singular incident marked a turning point for the agency. Through his own experience working on HIV in the early years of its emergence in Nigeria, the Minister was acutely aware of the need for a competent agency tasked with managing infectious disease outbreaks.

When I was appointed as the Chief Executive of NCDC by Mr President a few months later, it was a strong indication that the agency had come to stay, and the staff became more confident. However, upon my arrival, there was no enabling legislation from which to derive NCDC's mandate. This led to another significant challenge—a lack of consistent funding to keep the agency operational. In my determination to get to the root of the problem and chart a way forward, I discovered that the reasons for the resistance were often personal, rather than technical or professional. It was frustrating to see ego and power put before the best interests of the country. I tried some rapprochement with colleagues at the Ministry but realised very quickly, the depth of opposition from some of the directors.

A few weeks later, I attended the FMoH Top Management Committee (TMC) meetings to discuss issues concerning the health sector. The meetings usually began with me presenting an update on any new outbreaks of significance, but before I could speak, the Director of Public Health objected. She argued that her department, not NCDC, should be responsible for presenting the weekly epidemiology report. I was taken aback by her objection. The report had been prepared by NCDC staff, with painstaking effort and analysis, and it included extensive contextual information. I had prepared thoroughly for the presentation and expected to receive guidance and feedback from the TMC, and I was in the room. The open objection from the Director of Public Health surprised me, but I remained calm. All eyes were fixed on me. I could particularly feel the Director of Public Health's gaze drilling into my entire existence as though we were chronic rivals. I was speechless, and a seething anger began to bubble inside me. I recognised this plot—a power tussle, which I wasn't willing to engage. The Director of Public Health wanted to assert her authority, and she was willing to undermine NCDC to achieve this. I wasn't about to let that happen.

I took a deep breath and calmly explained why NCDC was best equipped to present the report, and how our expertise and knowledge would ensure that the presentation was comprehensive and accurate. Fortunately, the Minister, Professor Adewole, stepped in and overruled her objection. He made it clear that NCDC would present the report, and that was final. It was a small but significant victory, and it gave me the confidence to keep fighting for NCDC's place in the grand scheme of things.

Another bizarre example of this misplaced obstructionism was the Director of Public Health objecting to the National Reference Laboratory (NRL) hosting the implementation of a planned validation exercise of HIV rapid test kits. This was less than a year after we had successfully operationalised the laboratory; hosting such a large project would have provided several training opportunities for our staff. However, she insisted that the validation could take place in any other laboratory, except NCDC NRL. I couldn't understand what inspired this antagonism, and it was disheartening to see this level of destructive resentment by a public servant. She was, in fact, preventing the development of both our institutional and individual capacities, which was the exact opposite of her responsibility as a leader. It hurt to see our efforts hindered by those who should have been our allies. Still, we forged ahead. It was draining, but we persevered.

After these incidents, I made several attempts to reach out to the Director of Public Health, but she remained cold and unyielding. I decided to try a different approach. Instead of focusing on trying to win over the Director of Public Health, I began to build relationships with sister agencies and other departments within the ministry. Over time, they started to see that we were all on the same team, and we needed to work together to achieve our goals. The Director of Public Health remained distant. She never visited the agency during her tenure and was eventually promoted out of the ministry. I never quite figured out the reason for that level of antagonism towards me or NCDC. Nonetheless, I was happy with the progress we made on so many other fronts.

Whispers circulating along the corridors of the ministry indicated that I was a 'young' man who was 'pushing too hard' and not 'carrying everyone along.' I heard that I was considered an 'outsider,' and hadn't sufficiently 'humbled myself' to the 'elders' in the ministry. I reckoned these rumours were due to the generational difference between the 'old school' way of doing things and the more progressive and inclusive methods championed at NCDC. We, however, couldn't afford to concern ourselves with these distractions. I told my team, that we had a country to build, and we would do it our way.

In 2018, I wrote a piece titled *2017: A Year Like Never Before for Infectious Disease Outbreaks*, reflecting on the tough year that it had been. So many lives were lost to the cerebrospinal meningitis outbreak, and in the same year, we detected cases of yellow fever and monkeypox, two diseases that hadn't been seen in Nigeria for decades. The re-emergence of these diseases was concerning, but we knew that it was a sign that our surveillance systems were working better, detecting diseases that had most likely been circulating quietly for years; explaining this to the public was difficult. Also, governors were deeply unhappy that we were discovering outbreaks in their states, but we continued to improve our response. We used genomic sequencing and other epidemiological investigations to determine their source and contain their spread, detecting and responding to some of the worst disease outbreaks in the country's history. Our efforts undoubtedly saved lives. But I was aware of the human cost of these outbreaks and knew that there was still much work to be done.

At the beginning of my tenure, I encountered an unexpected challenge with the newly formed West African Regional Centre for Surveillance and Disease Control (RCSDC) and agency of the West African Health Organisation (WAHO). I was vaguely aware of the establishment of this new regional agency, but I wasn't briefed on it when I resumed at NCDC. Apparently, the previous Chief Executive of NCDC was asked to lead the RCSDC ad interim, and the responsibility wasn't formally handed over to me when I resumed. I approached Dr Crespin, the Director General of the West African Health Organisation (WAHO), to clarify things. He apologised for any confusion and oversight, after which I was made acting director. In this role, I was committed to fulfilling the mission of the RCSDC and worked diligently to ensure necessary resources were in place for its commencement. I helped secure a building for the agency's operations, ensuring that the Federal Government of Nigeria upheld its promise in this regard. It was a challenging but fulfilling experience, and I'm glad that I could contribute to the establishment of this important regional agency.

I appreciate the immense support and recognition Professor Isaac Adewole offered us at NCDC. He attributed this to the perspective he gained on his early visits to the UK's Public Health England and the US CDC where he saw first-hand, the importance of having a functional public health institute, which inspired him to create and support a similar infrastructure in Nigeria. Professor Adewole's backing of NCDC went beyond just words. He supported the mandate of NCDC as stated in the bill establishing it and supported it through the Senate and House of Representatives to Mr President. His strong leadership ensured that the agency grew and received its deserved respect, leading to more countries following Nigeria's lead in setting up a national public health institute.

In November 2018, I was attending a conference in Maputo, Mozambique when I received news that NCDC Act had finally been signed into law by Mr President. It was a long-awaited and hard-fought victory. I felt a mix of emotions: relief, joy, and gratitude. With the new Act in place, we could finally access the resources we needed and recruit personnel with specialised skills. Taking the Bill through the Senate and House of Representatives was a long journey, but we had the support of parliamentarians like Senators Mao Ohuabunwa, Samuel Anyanwu, and Honourable Mohammed Usman, who were committed to achieving this at a time NCDC wasn't the primary focus for most government officials. When COVID-19 arrived, many of the Senators and Representatives who had been hesitant about NCDC Act were proud of their role in getting it signed into law. Indeed, persistence and persuasion proved to be key instigators of change. Having a legal mandate has made an enormous difference in NCDC's ability to respond effectively and save lives, and it would have been difficult to achieve a cohesive response to the pandemic without a central coordinating agency.

NCDC didn't have an establishing Act when I was appointed as Chief Executive, thus, my appointment was tied to the tenure of the President. After the presidential elections in 2019, there was a delay in updating my appointment status despite the NCDC Act having been passed 6 months earlier. As a result, I was left in limbo—to continue in my role when the President's tenure expired or not? I brought this to the attention of the office of the Secretary to the Government of the Federation who managed these processes, but the reorganisation during the start of the President's second term caused delays. Irrespective of assurances from his office that I was expected to continue running the agency, rumours began to circulate, stating that I had 'refused' to step down when my 'tenure' expired. At this point, I had only been in office for two and a half years.

I sought advice from the President's office and was told to carry on until I received formal communication. It was difficult, but I remained focused and continued to work as best I could. An online article was published on a nondescript platform, raising concerns about the leadership of NCDC. It contained information that could only have been shared by colleagues within the agency. At this point, I realised that I needed to step back and allow things unfold. I decided to take some of my accumulated annual leave and spend time with family, giving the Presidency time to organise itself. A week later, I received official confirmation that I had been appointed for a five-year tenure as Director-General of NCDC by Mr President. I was grateful because this appointment put all circulating rumours and concerns to rest. More importantly, it allowed me refocus my energy and continue leading NCDC towards my vision for the agency.

Throughout my time in government, particularly during my time as Director General of NCDC, I have come to strongly believe that government institutions can indeed function effectively in Nigeria. The belief was founded not only on my personal experience, but also on the progress made at other agencies in the health sector, including NACA, NPHCDA, NIMR, and NIPRD. I'm particularly proud that the work we did at NCDC has been acknowledged by top political leaders in Nigeria, including the President, the Vice President, and several state governors. We persevered, and now, in 2023, NCDC is regarded as a model national public health agency, not just in Nigeria but also globally.

There were times I felt like a young rebel trying to shake things up in a conservative environment. I was appointed in my mid-forties, yet some people believed I was too young to hold an office of such importance. I drew strength from watching forty-year-old leaders in some of the world's largest economies, and I was determined to not let this bother me. I also had the support of a team of young and dynamic individuals, who shared my vision and were ready to work hard to make it happen. As an 'outsider' who had spent the previous 20 years working abroad, I was considered a misfit in the Nigerian public sector. I knew that I had to prove myself and earn the respect of my colleagues. I made a conscious effort to change this narrative with my actions, appearance, and language. But what really made a difference was our ability to deliver results and establish NCDC as one of the most respected public health agencies in the world.

The progress we made wasn't by chance; it was the result of strategic planning, hard work, and a commitment to excellence. I am always gladdened by updates from our dedicated staff, who have continued to progress in their careers. Their commitment to public health and their passion for building a stronger health system in Nigeria is truly inspiring. Under their watch, NCDC will make greater strides and serve as a model for other institutions in Nigeria and beyond.

23

NEW PARTNERSHIPS FOR HEALTH SECURITY

During the acute phase of the pandemic, on a typically hectic day at NCDC, I heard a lot of commotion outside. I peered out of my office window and saw a convoy of cars and a team of soldiers making their way into our campus, then headed towards the entrance to find out what was going on. The Director General of the National Youth Service Corps (NYSC), Brigadier General Shuaibu Ibrahim, had paid us an unexpected visit.

I was taken aback by the sudden arrival of a high-ranking military officer, but any reservations I had were quickly dispelled by General Ibrahim's calm and affable demeanour. He didn't waste time in stating the purpose of his visit, which was to express his concern regarding the impact of the pandemic on the NYSC programme. In addition to the work experience recent graduates obtain from the NYSC, young Nigerians in the programme are crucial to the survival of various sectors, including education and health. With the pandemic exacerbating existing backlogs, the need for extra human resources had become urgent.

General Ibrahim shared his vision for safely restarting the programme amidst the ongoing pandemic. His commitment to the NYSC and its mission moved me, and I was eager to help. This conversation marked the beginning of a fruitful partnership between NCDC and NYSC. We developed a comprehensive plan to ensure the smooth and safe reopening of NYSC camps. It was a big risk that could have backfired if it went wrong, but given the age group of those involved and their active involvement in mitigating the virus, I was confident we could pull this off. I was most confident in the General's personal commitment to making this happen.

Figure 26: Press Briefing with the DG, General Ibrahim to announce restart of the National Youth Service Scheme.
Photo credit: Ifeoluwa Ojo/IKP Studios

The collaboration of NCDC with NYSC evolved into a long-term relationship, one that would eventually lead to the development of a bespoke initiative for corps members to become public health champions—the IPC Vanguard Programme. Through the IPC Vanguard Programme, we trained 50 young corps members per camp to monitor adherence to public health and social measures, educate their peers, and participate in other activities that could help control the spread of infectious diseases in NYSC camps. I was impressed by the vivacity with which these young people stepped up to serve their country. Until I left NCDC, General Shuaibu and I continued to brainstorm ideas on how to move the country forward during these difficult times. It was an honour to work with such an extraordinary soldier who was passionate about serving our country and making a difference in the lives of young Nigerians.

The lockdown imposed in the early weeks of the pandemic had severely impacted businesses. Employees couldn't report to work, customers couldn't move freely, and the balance sheets were in real trouble. To overcome the impact of this pandemic, we needed all hands on deck. The emergence of CACOVID was, of course, the most prominent example of the private sector taking responsibility and stepping up to the challenge. But there were many other private sector initiatives supporting the COVID-19 response. An effective partnership with the private sector is not only about financial and material support; we can learn from their strengths in areas such as accelerated procurement processes, supply chain management, and the rapid deployment of resources. The private sector can bring valuable expertise and knowledge that can be utilised to strengthen our health security systems, but we have to be intentional about this.

I reached out to my friend Zouera, Managing Director of the Aliko Dangote Foundation, with a proposal for CACOVID to transition to a standing committee that would continue to support health security in Nigeria. She promised to get back to me, but I knew that they had moved on. In Nigeria, one is almost always preoccupied with the problem of the day. Zouera shared my vision and dedication to the cause, but we still have a long way to go in persuading other private sector leaders to prioritise health security, especially in the absence of a pandemic.

Another excellent partnership developed during the pandemic was with the Nigeria Armed Forces. Like in many countries, the military has exceptional infrastructure that could be used to support public health. Throughout the pandemic, we worked with different arms of the military to operationalise their medical laboratories for testing military personnel and their families. We developed a close and intensive working relationship, which allowed us to better understand each other's capabilities and potential areas for cooperation. From this collaboration, we realised that we had numerous other opportunities for partnership beyond testing of military personnel and their families. The alignment of priorities was critical, as it was necessary to ensure the military forces remained healthy and operational to carry out their work effectively.

The COVID-19 pandemic revealed that health security is also critical to national security. A tiny virus may appear inconspicuous, but it can wreak havoc on the nation's health, leaving it weak and vulnerable. Therefore, we must redefine 'security' to include health security as a critical component of national security. I'm extremely proud of the progress we made through this collaboration and excited about the exceptional work NCDC and the military will continue to do towards the improvement of public health in Nigeria.

Collaboration between the parastatals in the health sector—NPHCDA, NIMR, NACA NIPRD, and NAFDAC—also reached new heights during the pandemic. I remember when Dr Faisal Shuaib, the Executive Director of NPHCDA, called me to ask what we needed for the response. Without hesitation, he sent a team of technical personnel and vehicles, placing them entirely at the disposal of

NCDC. This act of generosity not only provided us with necessary resources but also strengthened our bond as colleagues and friends. We also worked closely with our counterparts at the institute of medical research, NIMR, to carry out the seroprevalence surveys in many states, taking advantage of their strong research focus and capabilities. Their expertise proved invaluable in understanding the prevalence of COVID-19 across the country.

For many years, we struggled with clearing emergency supplies donated to the country; we couldn't depend on organisations that had collected and shipped us supplies to also pay for the bureaucracy of the Nigerian ports, so we turned to colleagues at NAFDAC for help. We worked together during the pandemic to establish a faster clearance process. This was a huge relief, and it enabled us distribute these supplies to those who needed them most.

Another area we witnessed the value of collaboration was in the work with the National Institute for Pharmaceutical Research and Development (NIPRD). There were several apparent cures proposed for the treatment of COVID-19, and we wanted to ensure that all claims were appropriately validated. We invited NIPRD to lead this investigative process. By working together, we ensured that potential remedies or cures were properly investigated before use. While we didn't always agree on everything, we understood that we had to work together for the country's benefit.

Before the pandemic, we had strong ties with several international partners, and the number of connections grew over time. We collaborated with national public health agencies from different countries, including the US CDC, UK Health Security Agency, and Germany's Robert Koch Institute (RKI). These partnerships went beyond just supporting NCDC with funds. The agencies shared their extensive knowledge and experience gained over many years. Their support wasn't just financial; it was a valuable source of expertise that helped us deal with complex health issues. The collaboration with these institutions not only contributed to the growth of NCDC, but also strengthened our joint effort in contributing to global health security.

The relationship with the general public was one of the biggest wins during the pandemic. We recognised the importance of being transparent with the Nigerian people, even when the news wasn't good. The quick and efficient responses provided during the pandemic were crucial to building trust and credibility with the public. In contrast to other government agencies perceived as slow or unresponsive, NCDC used its platforms to inform and update the public about the response. Even now, people approach me at airports and restaurants, expressing their gratitude for the calm the NCDC team provided during one of the most uncertain times in our nation's history.

However, good communication couldn't solve all our problems. It was difficult to completely isolate ourselves from the declining trust in the government, especially with incidents such as the #EndSARS protests in Lagos and the worsening economy. The public's perception of the lack of empathy exhibited by many of the country's political leaders didn't help matters either. An example of an unforced error was the banning of Twitter for seven months during the pandemic. Young people were denied the opportunity to share their views, and many arms of the government lost the opportunity to share the work that they were doing, including NCDC.

Despite this, we continued to maintain transparency with Nigerians to preserve their trust in us. This required reinforced integration of NCDC's stakeholders, who helped us communicate NCDC's key messages even when we were offline.

As the number of reported COVID-19 cases and deaths in Nigeria began to decline in mid-2021, it felt like a weight was lifted off our shoulders. Lockdowns and restrictions had taken a toll on people's lives and livelihoods, and it was understandable that people were eager to move on and return to some semblance of normality. We now had a steady supply of vaccines, even though they came late and were insufficient for our large population.

The relative calm of this period gave us the opportunity to forge new relationships and partnerships that extended beyond the immediate focus on COVID-19. The pandemic wasn't only a health crisis but also a crisis of confidence for many Nigerians. It was also a turning point in the country's capacity to respond to outbreaks, and we couldn't afford to rest on our laurels. We had to continue building on the relationships we had established and use the lessons learnt from the pandemic to prepare for future outbreaks. I personally met with many leaders, brainstormed with my team, and identified areas of mutual interest. This helped us revitalise our partnership approach to include benefits for NCDC's partners. We needed them to see that it was also in their best interest to invest in Nigeria's health security. In the past, we often had to argue our case and explain the devastating impact outbreaks could have on our economy, businesses, and way of life. It wasn't always easy working with others, but it was always necessary to have a long-lasting impact.

The pandemic also highlighted the fragility of public health and healthcare delivery systems, and the need for a more robust and sustained approach to public health emergencies. As a result of the pandemic, many other public health challenges were exacerbated. For example, the disruptions to immunisation programmes have led to an increase in vaccine-preventable diseases. Women's access to reproductive health services have been severely impacted, with many unable to access the care they need. During the epidemic, there were more reports of domestic violence and mental health issues. All of these social issues were worsened by a pandemic that kept people separated and unable to obtain needed social care and assistance.

The good news is, there have been efforts to sustain the gains made from COVID-19 response efforts. A new bill was debated in the National Assembly to define a mechanism for sustaining the PTF structure and using it when multi-sectoral coordination was required at the highest level of government. We need sustained attention and resources directed towards public health emergencies. Structures like the PTF can provide the necessary coordination and leadership for a rapid response, especially across government. While this structure may not be appropriate for all outbreaks, it would certainly be useful for major outbreaks as well as humanitarian emergencies.

'An outbreak or emergency or crisis is not the time to start handing out business cards.' This adage that I picked up during my various work engagements has become a mantra, especially in the context of health security. It is important to remember that crises will inevitably occur, and when they do, we must be ready to collaborate effectively. It is not enough to simply have relationships on paper; we must actively cultivate and maintain them. The success of the response to COVID-19 was largely due to the relationships we had developed with other government agencies, the private sector, and the general public. It is my hope that these relationships continue to grow and thrive, serving as a model for how government agencies can collaborate to achieve common goals.

Figure 27: During one of our many appearances in the National Assembly. Photo credit: Ifeoluwa Ojo/IKP Studios

24

A FINAL FAREWELL

When I first joined NCDC in 2016, I was filled with excitement and a deep sense of purpose. I love my country deeply—sometimes more than I should—and absolutely relished the opportunity to serve and make a real difference. Many Nigerians will understand what I mean by 'more than I should.' Welcome to Nigeria, where the endless hurdles will leave you in a constant state of exhaustion—where one always has to swim against the current, forced to engage irrational battles that throw one's sanity into question. Yet, many Nigerians love this land very deeply, like I do.

As months and years passed, my commitment to NCDC only grew. Despite the long hours, the difficult decisions, and the countless obstacles that we faced, I never wavered in my dedication to the cause. For me, this was never just a job. I poured my heart and soul into it every day, always thinking about what was best for the organisation. I worked on Saturdays, Sundays and barely took annual leave—and I'm not saying this to get praise. I loved my job. Although I hardly thought about what direction to take my career after my tenure at NCDC, I did consider pursuing academic options, where I could reflect on my experiences, share them with others, and perhaps even write this book in a more peaceful environment.

The two years spent in the thick of the pandemic took a huge toll on me, and I'm sure it was the same for everyone directly involved in the response. I was grateful that our boys were able to continue their education, knowing that many children around the world were not as fortunate due to school closures. The daily responsibilities, public scrutiny, and constant fear of the unknown was intense. All these left me mentally exhausted, and I struggled to find time for those I cared about. In the middle of a pandemic, there was no time to slow down. Taking a break to breathe wasn't always an option.

Still, I could not help but feel a sense of quiet pride as I looked back on what we had achieved since starting at NCDC in 2016. Not only had we strengthened our country's public health capacities, we had also built trust among Nigerians. By 2021, NCDC had become one of the world's most respected public health institutions, receiving accolades from various sources and cited as a prime example of best practice.

I was excited about the progress John Nkengasong was driving in Africa CDC. Seeing people who look like you in leadership roles sends a clear message: you too can achieve great things. Representation dismantles barriers, creating a more inclusive and diverse society. Likewise, the early years of my career in Europe coincided with the emergence of the 'Africa Rising' narrative. I was inspired by the progress being made in many sectors on the continent, even though I knew that science and public health weren't 'rising' as rapidly. Africa, as a continent, needed to play a larger and more proactive role in shaping the evolution of global public health.

I remember being at WHO headquarters in Geneva after Dr Tedros was elected as the Director General of WHO—the first African

DG! Africans in the room were excited to see one of our own rise to such a respected position of leadership. I had long admired Dr Tedros for his unwavering dedication to public health, especially during the peak of the pandemic. We met several times in person, including his first official visit to NCDC in 2018.

One Saturday in June 2021, Dr Tedros called me while I was winding down after a stressful week. I was delighted albeit surprised. We exchanged pleasantries, and he buttressed his efforts to enhance WHO's operations, even amid a global pandemic. With the support of the German government, WHO was establishing a new hub in Berlin to improve data collection and analysis for better decision-making. And then came a shocking surprise. Dr Tedros wanted me to lead the new hub! What do you say when the Director General of WHO not only calls you, but also offers you an important job?

Dr Tedros complimented my work in Nigeria and wanted me to join his leadership team. It was an incredible honour and an opportunity to take my passion for public health to the global stage. I was both anxious and excited and my heart skipped a beat as he shared the opportunity with me in detail. He added that he had already spoken to the Chancellor of Germany, and she was excited about the prospect of me leading the new WHO Hub in Berlin. I could have jumped off my seat and said yes, but I gathered my thoughts and took a deep breath. In those few seconds, I considered three important constituencies I needed to carefully consider before making any decision. I calmly thanked Dr Tedros for his trust and confidence in me. I assured him that I was interested in joining his team but needed to consult with my family and Mr President.

When I got off the phone with Dr Tedros, I first thought of Vivianne and our two boys. Just five years ago, my family and I had made the profound decision to move back to Nigeria. We were just settling into our new life, building our home, and our boys were adjusting to their new school. Vivianne was building up Nigeria

Health Watch, the NGO she was leading, and now had a growing team of over 20 staff members at the time. Secondly, my team at NCDC was coming together. We had just completed a massive recruitment exercise resulting in a staff strength of over 500 core staff—five times the number of staff we had when I first took on the leadership role in 2016. Thirdly, I was appointed by the President, and I knew that I couldn't just resign in the middle of the pandemic. Mr President didn't speak a lot, but his few words were always of gratitude and support.

That evening, I shared the news with Vivianne. She remained her usual calm self, and with a knowing smile, assured me that we would reach a decision that would work for our family, no matter what. Looking back, I realise that many of the moves our family made in the more than 20 years we had been together had been unplanned. However, we were grateful for the opportunities that came our way and have always tried to make the most of them. We believe the places work took us always had a way of enriching our lives. Vivianne and I carefully considered the pros and cons of accepting the offer, weighing its impact on our personal and professional lives.

As I pondered the offer to join WHO leadership team, I considered what it meant for my current position at NCDC. The pandemic response was still ongoing but thankfully, the number of COVID-19 cases had declined and most of society had almost completely returned to business as usual. In fact, we were able to activate a cholera EOC due to the increasing number of cholera cases, while keeping the COVID-19 EOC in full response mode. A lot had changed in the past five years. When I first assumed leadership of NCDC, I was heavily involved in the day-to-day operations of the EOC. Now, thanks to the growth and development of our team, I could focus more on my leadership responsibilities, while the rest of the team took charge of the EOC meetings and operations. But this didn't make the decision to leave any easier. Nonetheless, I was confident they could carry on without me, given the strong foundation we had built.

Getting approval from Mr President was the hardest. I had to be discreet and find a way to approach him without drawing too much attention to myself; this wasn't very easy in Nigeria. Luckily, during the peak of the pandemic, our team's hard work had earned us some contacts at the Presidency. I started reaching out to them, hoping to arrange a discreet audience with the President. Before I could make any headway, I received another call from Dr Tedros. He had taken the liberty of calling his friend, the Minister of Foreign Affairs in Nigeria, Geoffrey Onyeama, whom he had worked with Ethiopia's Minister of Foreign Affairs. The Minister had then reached out to the President on my behalf, obtaining his approval. I was both relieved and impressed at how quickly things had fallen into place. But I still hoped for a direct approval from Mr President.

Figure 28: A final visit to His Excellency President Muhammadu Buhari

We arranged for an evening meeting at his residence to keep it away from the media. Near the end of my tenure, I was ready to meet Mr President alone for the first time. I was slightly nervous, but he put me at ease with his warm demeanour. He expressed his gratitude for my service to Nigeria and inquired about my family, making the conversation feel more like a friendly chat than a formal meeting. As I got ready to leave, he asked me to recommend a replacement for my position, which was a clear indication that my resignation had been approved. Mr President expressed his best wishes for my future endeavours. I thanked him and a photographer took a few pictures, capturing the moment for posterity.

I began talking to my close friends and advisors about the new role, seeking their advice and feedback. They were all enthusiastic and supportive, and I knew that it was time for me to take the next step in my career. But I had to keep this transition low-key and not let it become a distraction from the important work underway at NCDC. Thus, I continued to have these conversations quietly while juggling my other ongoing priorities.

On August 30 2021, one day before the Hub was inaugurated in Berlin, Germany, I found myself in the middle of a digital frenzy. An internal email sent to WHO staff announcing my appointment as head of the new WHO Hub for Pandemic and Epidemic Intelligence was in circulation. My phone buzzed with non-stop emails, messages, calls, and Twitter notifications. I was startled by the sudden influx of attention and had to turn off my phone. I hadn't even informed my team at NCDC. Later that evening, I composed an email to my staff, reassuring them that we still had a few months together, and I would do everything within my power to ensure a smooth transition for the organisation. It was a surreal experience—an exciting glimpse into what was to come in my new role.

On September 1 2021, I returned to Abuja to begin the final phase of our nearly six-year journey. It was essential to ensure continuity even during the transition process. We formed a small committee to ensure there were no loose ends in the handover process. Fortunately, within a few weeks, Mr President approved the appointment of Dr

Ifedayo Adetifa as the second Director General of NCDC. I was delighted to spend some time with him before his official resumption. We met partners together, emphasising the importance of continuity regardless of who was in charge. The good work must continue.

I made it a priority to ensure a detailed handover procedure. When I first joined NCDC, there was very little documentation available to guide me through the agency's daily operations, which made my onboarding very difficult. In a bid to not repeat past mistakes—I started working on my transition note. Over time, we had developed a culture of documenting and sharing progress over the years. Our financial reports were digitised, we had meticulously documented the details of our partnerships, and employee records were well annotated and preserved. With this foundation in place, I was able to write about my personal experience leading NCDC, sharing the highs and lows of the journey. Despite our huge progress, there was much to be done. With nearly 700 members of staff, we desperately needed a suitable location in Abuja to serve as NCDC's headquarters, a new warehouse, and space for the expansion of our National Reference Laboratory. There was more than enough work for the new DG.

During the transition period, I connected with as many NCDC staff as possible. I received multiple requests for one-on-one sessions and made time for each of them. I was inspired by how they described their own growth and their commitment to the organisation. In addition to the staff at NCDC, I was also pleasantly surprised by the outpouring of support from various groups and associations. From my secondary school and university alumni associations to the diplomatic corps in Abuja, many came together to honour my family and me with farewell receptions. It was humbling to see the impact our work at NCDC had on the wider community, and I felt grateful for the opportunity to have served Nigeria in this capacity.

Figure 29: Handing over NCDC to Dr Ifedayo Adetifa, the new Director General. Photo credit: Ifeoluwa Ojo/IKP Studios

Our departure was emotional. On the night I, together with Vivianne and our boys, boarded the plane, I couldn't help but feel a deep sense of nostalgia for Nigeria, our home. Although we were physically leaving Nigeria, our hearts and minds remained firmly rooted here. Our passion for making Nigeria and the African continent a better place transcends borders. I'm always thinking about how to inspire young people to pursue careers in science and how to encourage Africans working in universities around the world to return home and contribute to building capacity on the continent. There is so much work to be done. I firmly believe that Africa shouldn't just be passive consumers of research and development from other countries, but active contributors; hence, I saw my role at WHO as an opportunity to make an even greater impact on the continent.

On this note, I must say that I will always be proud of NCDC—the institution we had built with unquestionable passion and determination. I'm grateful for the opportunity to have served my country and my continent, and I look forward to making a bigger difference in the lives of people everywhere.

25

REFLECTIONS

My public health journey was hardly a well-defined path. When I graduated from the University of Nigeria in 1996, my focus was building a clinical career like most medical students. Public health wasn't on my radar. But over time, I understood the importance of addressing the underlying social determinants of health and the impact public health interventions could have on entire communities. Despite uninspiring and poorly delivered lectures on community medicine (as it was called at the time) at my medical college, I found myself eventually drawn to this field. After graduating from medical school, I was—like most of my peers—making plans on how to immigrate. Back then, the idea of public service in Nigeria wasn't very appealing especially for those who had options.

Any remnant thoughts of working in Nigeria dissipated when the political situation deteriorated. I finished university in the Abacha years, a difficult time to be optimistic about Nigeria's future. I left in search of professional and personal fulfilment. As I embarked on my journey abroad, I preserved my desire to make a positive impact in Nigeria's public health sector but had no idea how it would happen. I thought I was leaving behind all the chaos and frustrations, but I soon realised that Nigeria was engraved in the core of my existence. I stayed up to date with the latest news and happenings and made regular visits back home.

When our family had settled in the UK, I actively sought ways to re-engage with ongoing developments in Nigeria's health sector. One of the initiatives I co-curated with my good friend Ike Anya was *Nigeria: Partnership for Health,* a conference aimed at connecting like-minded Nigerians and experts to explore ways to improve the country's healthcare system. It was inspiring to see that many people shared our passion and enthusiasm for the cause. The events were always oversubscribed, and the rooms were filled with colleagues keen on developing Nigeria.

With a combination of perseverance and good luck, I ended up spending the most amazing five years at NCDC. Those five years were a truly transformative experience that opened my eyes to the complex inner workings of our country. They helped me understand, to some extent, why Nigeria wasn't fulfilling its potential. I found it interesting that we could achieve significant success at NCDC by working with the same public servants who were often the subject of Nigerians' contempt and criticism. The same group of people who were seemingly incapable of executing basic tasks became the driving force behind a model public sector organisation. This left me pondering the potential for change in Nigeria and how we can unlock it. How can we transform a seemingly broken system into one that works for all Nigerians?

At the beginning of my tenure at NCDC, I had to make a choice: take the easy way out and rely on external consultants or NGOs to get things done or try to work with the existing public servants. Some other parastatals had chosen the former. My new team was demotivated and disheartened by years of neglect and systemic issues—it would have been easy for me to give up and walk away, but this wasn't the right solution for NCDC. I had to try. These people, this team, hadn't failed Nigeria. Nigeria failed them. I would take a chance on them, and together we would try to turn this situation around. People are not always the problem. A lot of times, the system can simply not harness their fullest potential. We recruited the brightest minds out of university into public service, then failed to provide them with the support and resources to succeed. For most people working in the Nigerian civil service, there is often limited career development support or incentives to work and grow, not to mention the poor remuneration and working conditions. Employees had no expectations of themselves and were unsure of what was expected of them. We had to fix the system. This was the lasting solution.

Slowly but surely, our efforts yielded results. NCDC staff members began to see themselves as part of a team, as agents of change, and as leaders in their field. They worked long hours, often sacrificing their weekends and personal time, and did this with a sense of purpose and pride. They led response teams, got published in peer-reviewed journals, appeared on national television, and presented their work at major national and global conferences. They were sought after by regional organisations and international NGOs, and accepted into advanced professional development programmes all over the world. And as they grew, so did NCDC. We became a model for public service, a beacon of hope in a country that desperately needed it.

Witnessing this transformation was invigorating. For the first time, this promising team realised that the work they were doing actually mattered, which motivated them to work harder and smarter, to push themselves beyond their limits and take ownership of their work. They were no longer content with mediocrity. Excellence was the non-negotiable watchword. Of course, this transformation didn't happen overnight. It took a lot of hard work, dedication, and perseverance to get there. We witnessed the evolution of a group of Nigerians who had found their purpose and discovered they could make a difference. This discovery instigated a crucial paradigm shift.

I remember a TED Talk delivered by my friend Fred Swaniker, a Ghanaian entrepreneur and leadership development expert. In his talk, Fred spoke about the importance of leadership in places where institutions are weak, and the responsibilities of those in leadership. I kept this in mind as I tried to activate various leadership cadres within the organisation. The pervasive weakness and poor performance of public institutions in Nigeria was a hot topic of discussion, visible in the disarray of our airports, the chaos in our public universities, the corruption in our police force, and even in our electoral commission. Why do these institutions remain so weak despite repeated attempts at reform? This query is a central point of Nigeria's post-independence story, and it remains unanswered, to our collective dismay.

Nonetheless, watching NCDC staff thrive has been like watching a beautiful flower bloom. There are so many stories that I could tell about the journeys of many colleagues at NCDC, but one that comes to mind was that of a staff member who started as a storekeeper and has now completed a fully funded master's in public health at one of South Korea's top universities. After two years in South Korea, he has just returned to work in NCDC. There are many other stories like his, and these stories are a testament to what is possible when people are given the opportunity to grow and develop. Nothing gave me greater joy than seeing this happen.

I hope that these young people will continue to uphold the values they have imbibed and remain committed to building a stronger institution at NCDC. I know it's not easy, especially in a country where many are leaving in search of greener pastures. I often reflect on the recent *japa* trend—("*japa*" means to run away)—the emigration wave out of Nigeria. While it is heart-breaking, it is not new. There have been several waves of emigration in our history. However, I acknowledge that the current situation is particularly challenging, with widespread insecurity and a struggling economy. I can only hope that the government will take decisive action to address these issues and make staying in the country a viable option for its citizens. We can create an environment that encourages talented Nigerians to stay and contribute to the development of our country. We also need to make it easier for those who wish to return, by providing incentives, creating a conducive environment, and offering opportunities for personal and professional growth.

It is important to remember that the challenges we face are not unique to Nigeria. Every country has its own set of problems, and it is up to us to find creative and sustainable solutions to ours. We must keep building the country and the health sector of our dreams, one brick at a time. It won't be easy, but it is possible. As more young people begin to understand the potential impact they can have, I'm confident that we will see a brain gain and *japada* in this generation—a return to the country, just as our parents saw in theirs.

Reforming public institutions in Nigeria is not easy. I learnt this first-hand during my time at NCDC. The system is resistant to change, and those who push for reform are met with disdain from those who benefit from the status quo. With 20 years of experience working in national public health agencies around the world, I felt well-equipped to tackle the challenges at NCDC. Unfortunately, too few competent Nigerians are given the opportunity to lead our national assets. The political elites have little incentive to change this, as it does not serve their interests. Unless there is a radical shift in the people that citizens elect and what they represent, only few institutions will meet the expectations of Nigerians. The incentives for service are too few, and the incentives to do the opposite are inbuilt into the standard operating procedures. After five years at NCDC, I left with a few scars and bruises, but I'm proud of what we were able to achieve. We demonstrated that with perseverance and a 'street-wise' approach, it was possible to navigate the murky waters of public sector leadership and bring about positive change.

Figure 30: A late night shift in the office at NCDC.
Photo credit: Ifeoluwa Ojo/IKP Studios

When Mr President asked me for recommendations to fill my position at NCDC, I realised that finding the right person for the job wouldn't be easy. The next leader of NCDC had to be someone with an impeccable scientific background, as well as the confidence and charisma to adequately utilise their voice. The person would need to provide scientific advice to the Minister, and sometimes even the President, while recognising and accepting that political considerations often take precedence over scientific evidence. Additionally, NCDC needed a leader who could easily explain the fundamentals of our work to Nigerians and credibly represent the country on the global stage. A person brave and resolute enough to withstand the inevitable challenges they would face. After much deliberation, I recommended Ifedayo Adetifa. I was confident in his capacity and that he was the best candidate for the job.

To some, my appointment at WHO was seen as a departure from Nigeria for better opportunities. Many alleged that I had joined the *japa* generation. However, I knew that I wasn't being 'taken' away, nor was I fleeing. I knew that my role at WHO would allow me to amplify Africa's voice on the global stage. I knew I could never be 'taken' away from Nigeria. At about the same time, my friend John Nkengasong was appointed to a new role at PEPFAR after leading the Africa CDC. This was also met with the same narrative of Africa losing its best leaders. But I believe that our appointments are not a net loss for Africa, but an opportunity to take important African perspectives to the global health community. To truly achieve equity in global health, we need to have more African voices at the global decision-making table. It's not enough to simply advocate for equity from the sidelines; we must be present, actively shaping the conversation and decisions that affect our lives.

I'm grateful for the incredible love, support and mentorship I have received from other well-meaning Nigerians in this space, including Dr Ngozi Okonjo-Iweala, Amina Mohammed, Dr Akinwunmi Adesina, and Prof Muhammad Ali Pate. Like them, I have dedicated years of service to Nigeria. We are now in a privileged position to serve Nigeria and humanity from a global stage.

Figure 31: With Amina Mohammed during a visit to NCDC.
Photo credit: Ifeoluwa Ojo/IKP Studios

Lastly, I encourage Nigerians all over the world to cling on to the faith that Nigeria will be great. There is hope for us, and for our future generations. We may not be proudest right now, but the future is full of possibility. The good news is, we are collectively responsible for what it births. The power is in our hands, and our stories are ours to tell. We must rewrite the narratives that impede our growth and establish new prospects for change. I believe in us, despite it all.

God bless the Federal Republic of Nigeria.

FULL CIRCLE

Vivianne Ihekweazu

26

A PARTNER FOR ALL TIMES

With epidemics, the question is not if it will happen—but when.

As a result, countries are expected to maintain a high level of preparedness. This same advice is rarely given to communities, families, or individuals. The general public is not particularly aware of the threat of infectious disease outbreaks; warning signs are not included in any regular public health alert system to which people are exposed. At most, people are advised to stay healthy, maintain basic hygiene, and keep their living environments clean.

No community, family, or individual truly prepares for large epidemics or a pandemic. It was different for Chikwe and I. We were familiar with the threat of infectious disease outbreaks and had experienced them many times before through Chikwe's work. I think back to a year after we got married, I was pregnant and expecting our first child. As was often the case in the UK where we were living at the time, couples (well at least first-time parents) did the antenatal routine together.

During that early stage of my pregnancy, the opportunity came for Chikwe to support the response to an Ebola outbreak in Yambio, South Sudan. For many expecting couples, this opportunity would have been really ill-timed. Somehow, for me it made perfect sense, Chikwe was always keen on pursuing opportunities to build his experience. We were a young couple, I felt I could manage for the brief period he was away, so I was fully supportive of him travelling to Yambio, in South Sudan. However, it was so hard not having Chikwe around. Going to my initial antenatal appointments without him was a lonely experience, especially when most of the other women had their partners with them. But I took solace in knowing that he missed home. His occasional access to a satellite phone became a real novelty and the conversations we had alleviated my early pregnancy anxieties. By the time Ginika was born, Chikwe was back with me and the family unit started taking shape.

When news of a virus in Wuhan, China began to circulate in early January 2020, we knew enough to pay special attention, but like everyone else, we weren't quite sure where events would lead; there were so many unknowns. As news of escalating cases in Wuhan dominated the 24-hour news cycle on all channels, we too watched in utter disbelief. We wondered, could this really be happening?

I knew immediately that it looked like these initial 'events' would build up into something far greater than was initially imagined. Add to that, Chikwe was already being drawn into meetings both at the national and global level. At the same time, like many families, we were just settling back into a new year. We had just spent a wonderful Christmas in the village, although Chikwe was more distracted than usual. Following this, during the first week of January we spent a fantastic few days in Ponta do Ouro, Mozambique with some dear family friends.

When we moved back to Nigeria, we had pledged that we would find a way whenever possible to visit other African countries with our boys. I can't help but repeat an overused cliché, the African continent is truly blessed with so many beautiful countries to visit. We wanted to make sure that our boys remembered these images and experiences from different African countries. Plus of course, it offered us the opportunity to spend quality time with Chikwe where his focus was very much on us and the boys.

In late January 2020, Chikwe and I travelled to London so that Chikwe could fulfil his role with *The Lancet* Nigeria Commission, an important committee focused on providing actionable recommendations for achieving Universal Health Coverage in Nigeria. During that trip, I recall watching BBC News and listening to reporters discuss travel restrictions for people coming in from China. At the time, it seemed impossible to envision how restrictions to the UK, especially from China, would work. Just imagining the economic implications of such a ban was staggering.

Events continued to unfold and in early February Chikwe was invited as part of a WHO delegation on a fact-finding mission to China. I was anxious and we were quite hesitant to tell other members of our family about his trip. The news cycle at the time was showing people in hospitals on ventilators and now quite literally, Chikwe, again was going into the eye of the storm. Following his trip in 2004 to Yambio, South Sudan, Chikwe continued to work in many outbreak settings. I recall particularly another one that caused a lot of anxiety was his travel to Liberia to support the response to the large Ebola outbreak there. Why was this my husband always travelling to these outbreak hotspots? That was just who he was, it was his job and I respected what it meant to him. At least during the mission to Liberia, I was not expecting, however, we had two boys in primary school. We chose not to tell them where Chikwe was travelling to. Living in South Africa at the time, the country felt so far removed from the outbreak and we just did not want our boys to face any stigma if it came out that their dad had travelled to Liberia where the Ebola outbreak had already claimed countless lives.

Nonetheless, the seeming impossible happened, and other countries followed suit and travel restrictions were placed on passengers travelling from China. At this time, the Nigerian government was under so much pressure to close it borders for fear of the virus crossing our borders. However, we know that infectious disease outbreaks do not respect borders. Chikwe was constantly on the phone and started coming home late from work, even later each day, exhausted by the heightened anxiety in the country. Even when he got home, he was always on the phone. However, I did my best to try and provide normalcy within our home and I never went to bed before Chikwe got home. How could I? It was an opportunity for him to de-pressurise and unwind. There were so many false alarms and I quickly got to recognise the voices of people he spoke to regularly on the phone. Many I would meet in person later.

Figure 32: On several occasions our sitting room turned into a makeshift TV studio.

Thursday February 27, the first case of COVID-19 was reported in Nigeria. We did not sleep that night. Chikwe did not panic. Well, Chikwe does not often panic and quite frankly neither did I. We both knew that this was it. What happened in the next few hours was going to shape how the country responded to the news. Chikwe, with sheer clarity of mind knew that it would be critical to communicate the news to the Nigerian public and by default the global community. This was not a drill. Chikwe knew that he will have to work on this press release himself, it could not be delegated. This one was different. He asked me to review it, with an eye to how each sentence would be read, which I did, and he made some further edits. It was ready. His team was waiting to finalise the distribution to media houses and social media. All these happened on the dining table of our sitting room around midnight.

Building trust at this early stage was very important. I work in the communications space, so I knew that we had to get ahead of the news cycle and communicate the facts, in case the news leaked. Any miscommunication could have led to widespread panic. We had a small window and had to maximise it, there was a lot at stake. I could read the draft press release from the point of view of an enlightened citizen and detect when a press release sounded authentic. At this early stage, it was important as was the case throughout the response to be open, transparent and sincere with the public. It was as if Chikwe had prepared for this moment all his life. He was ready.

There was little time to get much sleep once the press release was finally shared. When our boys woke up the next morning, we told them the news. We have always ensured that we are open with them, trying to respond to any questions they have with the full maturity of growing teenagers. Seeing that neither Chikwe nor myself seemed to be panicking, they took the news in their stride and went off to school as usual. Of course, the news was repeated at their school and suddenly their father was thrust into the spotlight.

By March 23, Nigeria closed its land borders. We were shut in, confronted with an unprecedented occurrence that neither Chikwe nor I had ever experienced. The pandemic was upon us, and it was about to test the limits of everything that had begun for us as a family four years prior, when we moved home to Nigeria.

In June 2016, we were still living in Johannesburg, South Africa. I returned home from work to find Chikwe still in the pyjamas that I had left him in, earlier in the day. Our family had been in South Africa for five and a half years, and we had decided a year before that we would consider relocating to Nigeria, but we had our anxieties. Chikwe had already begun testing the waters, taking increasing trips home working on a few consulting opportunities. In anticipation of an eventual move, we had moved out of our home a month before our departure and were staying in the guest house of our good friends, Michael and Sheila Charles. With everything packed up and ready for the move back home, there was no turning back.

On the day that the news came, Chikwe's phone kept ringing. He took the calls one after the other, with his laptop in front of him. He appeared more preoccupied than usual as the calls flooded his line. Chikwe was unusually distracted, but when he had a brief pause between phone calls, he gave me that knowing look. Something was up—not necessarily something bad, though. Apparently, there was to be a major change in our well-laid plans.

While holding a ringing phone in one hand, he gently broke the news. He had just been appointed to lead the Nigeria Centre for Disease Control.

So, this was why the phone had not stopped ringing. It was the barrage of people who had been calling to congratulate him!!!

How was this possible?

The turn of events seemed so strange. I didn't remember discussing any of it. Had we talked about his applying for the role and I had merely forgotten? I suspended my disbelief and immediately asked, "Did you receive a phone call inviting you to take on the role? How did people find out about the appointment? When does the new role start?"

Details were scant at the time, and even Chikwe didn't have all the answers. All we had was a newspaper announcement. This was the basis for all the frenzy.

A month later, we were back in Nigeria. Chikwe was thrown right into the thick of running NCDC as soon as we arrived. He would frequently share his daily challenges—of which there were many—from the limited funds available for a national public health institute capable of meeting the needs of Nigeria's burgeoning population, to the team he was just getting to know, and we would have lengthy discussions about what he felt he needed to do, and his vision of the strategic direction of the organisation.

I was fortunate to continue working remotely at the time, so while Chikwe was busy with NCDC, I concentrated on settling our two boys into their new schools and adjusting to life in Abuja. This gave us some initial stability, even as I was also having to make significant changes in my life. Still, none of it was new to me; I had moved around and lived in various cities, so I was able to adjust. This time it was different though. Chikwe hadn't only taken on a new job, he was building the agency from almost ground zero. It required very long hours, frequent travel, and nearly all his free time. With great power comes great responsibility. This was very much the case for Chikwe in his initial role as the Chief Executive Officer of NCDC, given at the time the agency had no legal mandate. Chikwe's deep sense of responsibility meant that he very quickly took on the role with full vigour.

Given his leadership role in a government institution, Chikwe quickly recruited a team to support him. I can't say that we were totally prepared for this sudden change, however this brought many new people into our lives and it made us appreciate the times when we were alone as a family and could enjoy some privacy. I describe this as the "theatre" that comes with leadership positions in government.

Chikwe took this all in his stride and eventually gave up insisting that he wanted to carry his own bag, there were bigger battles to fight, he told me. However, he took this responsibility very seriously as he knew that he was there to 'serve' the public, and wanted to show that it was possible to do so. He would often say that there was no penalty for failure in the public sector. Expectations were low, so if you underperformed no one would hold you accountable. Having never worked in the public sector, this lack of accountability was totally alien to me.

We tried to find room for downtime with the boys, despite Chikwe's very busy schedule including a trip to the village the December before the pandemic. By then, I had transitioned to leading Nigeria Health Watch, a health communication and advocacy organisation based in Abuja. Some of our work focused on advocacy for epidemic preparedness funding, and the need to strengthen the country's health security architecture, so I was very aware of the critical gaps that existed in funding the health security needs of our country. How do you convince our leaders to prioritise something they can't imagine or fully understand? There is no ribbon cutting ceremony that enables our elected officials to boast if they allocate funds that help the country prevent a disease outbreak. For this reason, in the beginning, it felt like there was no real sense of urgency around ensuring that our national public health institute was adequately funded. Nigeria's needs are numerous, and our resources limited. Decision makers prioritised what was more visible to them and where they could get the greatest applause. After all, did Nigeria not beat Ebola?

Several days before the Chief of Staff tested positive in March 2020, Chikwe and other members of the Presidential Task Force on COVID-19 had been in meetings with him. As a precautionary measure, we decided that Chikwe would sleep in the guest room to protect me and our kids. There was so much going on at the time. At this early stage, the outbreak's trajectory was unknown, and we had to adopt all possible precautionary measures. I remember waking up the next morning feeling quite strange having my husband in the house, but in a different room. I would sit in a chair outside the guest room door and speak to Chikwe, never going near him. It really was quite bizarre for us and during this time, Chikwe still had to maintain full focus on the response. The phone calls and deluge of emails never stopped.

Our boys were initially worried, wondering why their dad was suddenly in a different room; perhaps, we had an argument? The new arrangement was quite unusual for them, and they were unsure of what to make of it. They were in the same house as their father, but they couldn't walk into the guest room and hug him. We tried to calm their anxieties, and after a while, they stopped probing and trusted what we told them. They immediately became accustomed to speaking to him from a distance or through a closed door. Being in self-isolation in the same house was really hard. We were so relieved when Chikwe tested negative at the end of the mandated quarantine period.

Our life had been disrupted, and I was starting to forget what our normal life looked like. Prior to the COVID-19 outbreak, despite his hectic schedule, he would come home on Friday night and I imagined he would be exhausted after another long and endless week. But he was often ready to end the week on a fun note. "Let's go out! I have agreed with some of my boys that we would meet up." There is nothing that Chikwe has always enjoyed, more than spending time with his boys. For him, this is a time when he can just be 'Chikwe'. Not 'Oga', or 'DG' or 'Sah'. He can be just another one of the boys. We would come home in the early hours of the morning and while in one of the few Abuja locations that we enjoyed, nobody paid much attention to us, and this is just how we liked it. We would be in a small group of friends, oblivious to those around.

I was conscious that, at the onset of the pandemic, the reality in countless families was having to deal with abrupt changes. From working at home, to home-schooling children. We all had to make very quick adjustments.

I'm not sure how much sleep Chikwe got in those days. It was clear that the pressure was really getting to him. He would be physically present, but mentally burdened and absent sometimes. Then there were the non-stop phone calls. Everybody vying for his attention. When some of our leaders needed testing, they would call him directly because they trusted in his ability to be discreet. Listening to him on the phone, I could tell by his reassuring words that many of our leaders trusted his wisdom and guidance and sought his advice. They felt comfortable exposing their vulnerability.

I have always known Chikwe for his *'broad shoulders'*—his unique ability to accommodate the many demands for his attention. He seemed to take it all in his stride. Despite the obvious weight that was placed on him, he made the burden appear light. My role was always to be strong and supportive in any way I could and I did my best not to falter at any time, but it was hard. I soon got an opportunity to support him in a different capacity than as his life partner.

With NCDC suddenly thrust into the spotlight, communication with the public became critical. Communication material, such as guidelines tailored to the Nigerian context, needed to be developed quickly. NCDC team was already dealing with the many demands of the outbreak response, so I offered to help with the development of some of the required guidelines. Shortly after, I worked with the relevant teams in NCDC, supporting the development of the 'Guidelines for Businesses and Schools' as well as for pregnant and lactating mothers. I realised that issues disproportionately affecting women weren't given the necessary focus or priority during the pandemic and were often overlooked. We collated all the available evidence from the WHO website, from peer-reviewed journals and other international public health organisations, but then critically adapted them to the Nigerian context. These guidelines were internally reviewed by NCDC and its development partners and finalised before dissemination.

Eventually, the need for more manpower at the early stage of the pandemic became evident. The agency was already responding to existing infectious disease outbreaks, such as Lassa fever and cholera, and the COVID-19 pandemic was a real spanner in the works. All NCDC employees had their hands full; hence, Nigeria Health Watch was invited to join the Crisis and Emergency Risk Communication team on a pro-bono basis to assist with communications.

The crisis communications team was divided into several functions, ranging from creating infographics based on messaging priorities, writing editorial published in newspapers, to assisting the fact-checking team. Together with two other members of my team, I joined this well-coordinated crisis communications structure.

I worked in the team that met weekly to assess and determine messaging priorities for the country, using data from social media, NCDC's rumour management system, and other data touch points. Together, we would share our thoughts on where we felt there were gaps in communication, assessing potential areas of miscommunication. This informed infographics, topics discussed during media interviews, information, education and communication

(IEC) material, and articles written by our smaller editorial sub-team. The editorial was then distributed to major print publications that published the articles, bolstering the response to the COVID-19 pandemic with evidence-based materials. The messaging priorities were also shared with the state health promoters who would then use them in shaping their communication. The idea was to have a unified message, however tailored to the local community context.

Working with the crisis communication team provided a clearer understanding of NCDC's response to COVID-19, as well as first-hand experience of the daily challenges and pressures Chikwe was facing. This was extremely beneficial to both of us during that difficult time. It got to a point for us that each morning felt like Groundhog Day; the previous day just seemed to infinitely repeat itself, and burnout began to creep in. I could tell that Chikwe was getting exhausted, but he had to muster all of his energy to keep going. To alleviate the pressure, we decided to get him a second phone because of the volume of phone calls he was receiving. This meant he could effectively respond to the most important calls. Nonetheless, the number of phone calls he received every day remained overwhelming.

Soon, when people were unable to reach Chikwe, and aware of my very obvious proximity to him, they started calling me. Most of these calls were from people we knew, well meaning, who genuinely wanted to assist with the response as they were aware of the pressures the agency was facing. We had to devise a method to properly engage and manage any offered assistance.

I focused on highlighting key areas where NCDC required urgent attention and determining whether the assistance offered aligned with NCDC's needs. If they did, I would refer them to the people at NCDC for follow-up. Chikwe had a limited window in which I could engage him in the early months of the pandemic, so I had to filter the messages I passed to him from the most critical—such as when a major telecommunication company was seeking to bolster the infrastructure in NCDC Connect Centre—to those outside NCDC's mandate.

I also witnessed incredible generosity and the formation of communities in response to the crisis. People wanted to help. People wanted to do whatever was in their power to support the response. During times of crisis, we often witness people's true humanity. In late March 2020, one of many WhatsApp groups was created. I was suddenly included in this group. It was called "Creatives Against COVID-19" and had over 30 members. The group included individuals like Ed Keazor and Obi Asika, as well as a variety of graphic designers, photographers, and film and documentary producers.

Nigeria's creative industry has evolved into a thriving sector, showing great talent that competes with the best in the world; it has self-organised and transformed into a dynamic economic powerhouse in the country. Its growth demonstrates the resourcefulness and resilience of Nigerian creatives, who have used local culture and digital innovation to make a significant impact both locally and internationally.

People in the group created COVID-19 advisory messages using infographics, animations, and banners, which they shared extensively throughout their different platforms. It was heartening that my opinion was sought on whether the messages were suitable. I frequently made the effort to bring them up to speed on what messaging priorities were being prioritised in any particular week. This influenced the creation of the material for advisory messages.

The late nights began to wear on us. I was now working seven days a week, round the clock, in addition to my work at Nigeria Health Watch and ensuring that our boys were okay, as I had to be mindful of how they were coping. The transition from in-person teaching to online education wasn't easy for parents, teachers, or students, and we were only fortunate that our children's school had already implemented Google Classrooms. Students submitted their homework using the platform, while teachers shared notes and classroom notices. I wouldn't say the adjustment was particularly easy for our children, but they were both in secondary school and somewhat independent.

However, most students in Nigeria couldn't access online education. For schools that adopted online schooling, parents were suddenly confronted with the unanticipated expense of ensuring that each of their children had their own laptop or other similar electronic devices to access educational material. Data shows that many students fell behind during this period, and many are still struggling to catch up. We also had to help our children cope with the mental isolation of online schooling and the loss of their ability to socialise and interact with friends. You can imagine how tough this was for young teenagers who were accustomed to hanging out with their friends. Many parents (often mothers) suddenly had to adopt the schoolteacher role, in addition to other roles. This was even harder for parents whose children were in primary school.

Chikwe's hectic schedule meant that often, he only saw the boys very briefly each morning before they left for school. By the time he came home each evening, rarely before midnight, the boys were fast asleep. We would often watch the daily Presidential Task Force on COVID-19, press briefings, and this way, the boys could see their dad while also understanding the progression of the outbreak and what Chikwe focused on. In a strange way, the boys were often asked about the outbreak at school. So, in their own way, based on their level of understanding, they were able to respond to their friends. It was also during these press briefings that Nigerians in the country and the diaspora got to know Chikwe. His words clearly inspired trust. To this day, people still recognise him and approach him to thank him for everything he did throughout the response.

The months that followed the first reported case in Nigeria taught me that unwavering support entails more than simply changing plans and relocating to another country. It means accepting that nothing is predictable and learning to cope with the uncertainty, while working together as a team—riding the ebbs and flows of change, knowing you have each other's back. Luckily, I've been somewhat able to continue in my career path regardless of where life took us. But I've also seen how an unpredictable life can have a negative impact on women. Having a husband who has to relocate from one country to another may seem exciting, but as a wife, you find yourself having to adjust almost at the drop of a hat. You learn not only to make sudden changes, but also take on the laborious responsibility of ensuring that wherever you move to, the transition is seamless for the whole family, especially when children are involved. Chikwe's appointment to NCDC was no different.

Figure 33: Chikwe was invited to the virtual Closing Gong ceremony of the Nigerian Stock Exchange in December 2020 (we became quite good at improvising his set-up for virtual meetings).

It has been a life-changing and immersive experience. It has opened many doors we never expected to open, while providing opportunities for us to find common ground in the work we do together and independently. We have always tried to make the best of any situation we encounter, and that will never change. It's onward and upward for us—yesterday, today, and always.

Figure 34: Premier of the documentary Unmasked: Leadership, Trust and the COVID-19 Pandemic in Nigeria.

27

HOPE AND OPTIMISM FOR THE JOURNEY AHEAD

Our return to Europe feels so familiar, like a journey that has gone full circle. This time though, returning about 20 years later, we are older and hopefully wiser—no longer at the beginning of our life together, but in the thick of things, with years of experience and teenage children to share it with. There are still unexpected and unpredictable changes, but there are also many undiscovered opportunities ahead of us.

Chikwe began his formal career in Berlin after getting his master's degree and post-qualification as a medical doctor and later moved to the UK to begin his public health training in Stonehouse, Gloucestershire. I was living in London. Back then, Chikwe made frequent, short-term trips to respond to public health emergencies. In those early days, I understood why public health meant so much to him, and why he chose to leave clinical practice. He always felt that he could be more effective solving public health challenges at a population level.

Coming from a background in development economics, I'm all too familiar with the impact of economic policies on the health sector in Africa, particularly Nigeria. The inconvenient truth remains that the Structural Adjustment Programme (SAP) in the 1980s, which aimed to reduce the role of government, resulted in a decrease in government spending in many sectors, especially healthcare. The underinvestment in health was the beginning of the brain drain, as the poor remuneration and working conditions in the public sector drove many health workers to seek employment opportunities in the private sector or leave the country entirely.

This historical context is worth highlighting because when we analyse the state of our health sector today, we see that our core health challenges consequently remain unchanged. As a result of historically inadequate funding for our health sector, the first known case of COVID-19 in Nigeria was detected in a state whose laboratory infrastructure was underdeveloped. This has always been a pain point, the lack of understanding that avoiding epidemics requires funding to ensure that we have effective surveillance systems across all states, as well as the health workforce necessary to detect and respond to frequent outbreaks. Following the emergency release of funds, the rollout of the laboratory infrastructure in the states began, which also included the construction of isolation units within existing Federal Medical Centres.

While Nigeria can be said to have overcome the pandemic, it drastically affected our economy, and the international migration of health workers has intensified. Nigeria is certainly not alone in this situation, but the consequences in the country are far-reaching. The doctor-patient ratio is estimated to be 1:5,000, compared to WHO's recommended 1:600. As a result, when Chikwe's appointment to WHO was announced, there were murmurs that we were losing another skilled medical professional. In two ways, I believe this conclusion is an incomplete reflection of the realities we face in Nigeria.

Firstly, the existential threat to our healthcare system is not simply a 'brain drain' as it is often described—more like a 'brain draw.' Talented individuals are drawn, or 'pulled' to other countries. The 'pull factors' are well understood. For many they want improved working conditions, better-equipped healthcare facilities, higher pay, and more training opportunities. This basically refers to people wanting to work in an environment where they can meet their basic needs while still pursuing their career goals.

Rather than engage in several, unyielding debates, we need to effectively address the factors contributing to the immigration of Nigerian healthcare professionals. Secondly, historically, global health has reflected the needs and priorities of high-income countries (which encompasses regions, such as North America, Europe, and Australia) with very little representation and inclusion of health professionals or policymakers from the low-and middle-income countries.

This migration is not being experienced by the health sector alone. Others in banking and telecoms are also migrating en masse. It is therefore not enough for decision makers to cast blame while wringing their hands. It is time to scrutinise this issue from a much broader perspective, including training more health professionals and a return to strengthening our education sector, especially basic education. Nigeria has a young population that is expanding. The median age is around 18 years old, which should be a benefit because we are harbouring a productive population, yet we are falling behind.

Having led Nigeria Health Watch and been the beneficiary of young people leaving our universities, I can say we are at the coalface of our country's education policy. I've observed that many graduates are unprepared for the workforce when compared to their peers in other countries. Yes, providing mentorships and opportunities for young people is important, but no one is entitled to this. Young people must also be willing to seek out these opportunities and prepared to do whatever it takes to learn more about their areas of interest. Organisations should also be bold in offering opportunities to these young people to enable them cut their professional teeth and help them build their 'career capital'.

Nigeria has incredibly bright young minds, which makes me very optimistic for our country. But with our fast-growing population and a slowing economy, opportunities are few and far between. There must be avenues for creating on-the-job training for young people. During a conference convened by the Nigerian Economic Summit Group (NESG) in 2022, there were proposals on how to improve the Nigerian education system, particularly stating the need to revisit our current education paradigm in light of our country's realities. This includes not just strengthening the foundational education level, but also rethinking higher education. People should be able to finish secondary education and immediately begin working and receiving on-the-job training, while pursuing a college degree. In addition, there should be a larger emphasis on teaching entrepreneurship as part of secondary education. It would be great to see more philanthropic investment in our education sector.

We only have one country, and it is in our collective interest to build it. Given the country's current challenges, this may appear naïve and idealistic; however, I'm certain there are many lessons to be learnt from the establishment of NCDC, a nascent government agency that faced one of its most difficult challenges at a critical time in this country's history. Many of the 'foot soldiers' that travelled across the country during the critical phase of the response were an army of young and dedicated health workers. This demonstrates what is possible when our youth are actively engaged and empowered. I continue to witness this energy at Nigeria Health Watch, which provides a safe environment for young people to refine their skills, learn, and thrive.

It is this idealism, together with consistent family support, that has enabled us to accomplish whatever we have. Family matters under all circumstances and underpins everything that we do. With family, no storm is too great to overcome.

Figure 35: Proud moment, as I recieved the national order of Officer of the Order of the Niger (OON) on Chikwe's behalf from President Muhammadu Buhari, in October 2022
Photo credit: Bayo Omoboriowo

ACKNOWLEDGMENTS

As we were thrown into the middle of the pandemic, we recognised very early that we had a responsibility to write this book. Almost every day, there were events happening around us, some big and some mundane, that were shaping the future of our country and the world, and we were in the middle of it all. However, 'wanting to' and 'doing it' are two different things. Somehow, with the encouragement of many of our loved ones, we put our thoughts to paper.

We are truly overwhelmed with appreciation for everyone who encouraged us to keep going on this journey, to tell our story of the pandemic, and of the institution that led the response, as well as the personal story that accompanied it. Our heartfelt thanks goes out to everyone who helped, encouraged, and supported us while we worked on this book. Thank you for your patience when we did not spend as much time with you as we would have loved to while we were at it. This journey did not begin while we were writing this book, nor will it end with it—but it continues as we learn every day.

First and foremost, we want to thank our family, our parents, both those who are still with us and those watching over us. We both have parents that encouraged intellectual curiosity as we grew up, as well as a strong sense of family. To our siblings, Christine, Adaoha, Anthony, Edozie, Felix and Rosemary, as well as their other halves, Chijioke, Keri, Ukaoma, Chi Chi and Rich, and our beloved nieces, nephews, and godchildren—you make our lives complete.

To the many friends and mentors whose unwavering belief has been a constant source of inspiration. The many colleagues with whom Chikwe worked at the Robert Koch Institute in Germany, the Health Protection Agency in the UK and the National Institute of Communicable Diseases in South Africa. Special thanks to James Stuart who in the early days helped make Stonehouse in Gloucestershire a home and a place to learn, welcoming us to his family. To Ibrahim Abubakar, whose brotherhood has never wavered since we met in London, and Lucille Blumberg for the warm welcome to South Africa and camaraderie since.

To Ike Anya, who loves books, urged us to write and was one of the first people to cast a critical eye on our book. To Nancy Adimora whom we are not only tremendously proud of but who guided us through the process of bringing this book to where we needed it to be. Moky Makura, you have inspired us in so many ways and always emphasised the importance of telling and owning our own narrative.

We are grateful to our friends who kept calling to check on us during the difficult times, during the onset of the pandemic, offering their support in any way they could, and encouraging us to keep pushing. To Michael and Sheila Charles, whose boys strengthened the spirit of true brotherhood with our boys, during a period when social isolation became so difficult for them.

Thank you, especially to NCDC team, who showed the world and themselves what true public service means. From the junior staff to the directors, who gave so much of themselves every day to the mission. By your work and attitude, we defined for ourselves what a highly efficient parastatal feels like, defying conventional wisdom about public service in Nigeria. To the Nigeria Health Watch team, '*teamwork makes the dream work*' every day of the week.

Special thanks to our publishers, Masobe Books. We are so proud of the work that you are doing with literature on the continent, and grateful for the incredible support in bringing our narrative to life.

Finally, many thanks to the readers of this book. We hope that by sharing our story, you will be inspired to strive for more than you think is possible. When presented with difficult situations, you would be surprised at how strong and resilient we can be.

We are incredibly grateful for the opportunity of public service—there is no greater honour than to serve one's country. For the Nigerians reading this book, we implore you not to give up on building the country of our dreams.

Chikwe and Vivianne

ABOUT THE AUTHORS

Chikwe Ihekweazu is an infectious disease epidemiologist and public health leader with over 25 years of experience in senior leadership roles at the World Health Organisation, the Nigeria Centre for Disease Control, the South African National Institute for Communicable Diseases, the UK's Health Protection Agency (HPA), and Germany's Robert Koch Institute. He is the recipient of the Officer of the Order of the Niger (OON) awarded by the President of the Federal Republic of Nigeria, for his service.

Vivianne Ihekweazu is an accomplished health communications professional with over 20 years of experience. As the Managing Director of Nigeria Health Watch, a health communication and advocacy organisation based in Nigeria, she works tirelessly to structure health communications strategies that strengthen health advocacy in Nigeria. Using informed commentary, intelligence and insights on the Nigerian health Sector, she drives change on topics that matter to her including nutrition, maternal newborn and child health, routine immunisation, sexual and reproductive health & rights and health security.